# AN INTRODUCTION TO
## MYSTICISM

A. M. D. G.

# AN INTRODUCTION TO
# MYSTICISM

First published as
*An Introduction to the History of Mysticism*

by
Margaret Smith

New York
Oxford University Press
1977

Printed in Great Britain

# CONTENTS

# CHAPTER IX

# CHAPTER X

# CHAPTER XI

# AN INTRODUCTION TO
# MYSTICISM

# CHAPTER I

## THE NATURE AND MEANING OF
## MYSTICISM

THE word " Mysticism " itself comes down to us from the Greeks and is derived from a root meaning " to close." The mystic was one who had been initiated into the esoteric knowledge of Divine things, and upon whom was laid the necessity of keeping silence concerning his sacred knowledge. The term " mystical," then, might be applied to any secret cult revealed only to the initiated. The philosophers took over the word from the priests and applied it to their own speculative doctrines and thence it passed over into the Christian Church, which held itself to be a body of initiates into a truth not possessed by mankind at large. The derivation of the word was later held to give it the meaning of closing the mind to the influence of all external things, so that it might be withdrawn into itself, and so be fitted to receive the Divine Illumination.

But the real meaning of the word, as we use it now, represents something much wider than its derivation. That for which it stands is a tendency not limited to the Greeks, either priests or philosophers, nor bounded by the far-reaching comprehensiveness of the Christian Church. It denotes something which is to be found, in a highly developed state, in the early religious doctrines of the East ; in the Vedic literature ;

in Buddhism both in India and in China ; in a form strangely attractive, considering the apparently barren soil in which this flower has bloomed, in Ṣūfism, the mysticism of Islam, which has spread itself and taken firm root in Persia, Turkey and India as well as in Arab lands ; in Judaism, again an unpromising environment, to all appearances ; and finally, as we have seen, in Greece and in the West.

It seems plain that a mystical doctrine found at an early period in the world's history, developing and persisting through the centuries, so that at one and the same time we find it, in an almost identical form, in the religions of the East, in the Western Christianity of Germany, France and Italy and in the Byzantine Church of Constantinople, represents a spiritual tendency which is universal, a tendency of the human soul which is eternal.   As a great Oriental scholar [1] has expressed it :

" There is hardly any soil, be it ever so barren, where Mysticism will not strike root ; hardly any creed, however formal, round which it will not twine itself.   It is, indeed, the eternal cry of the human soul for rest ; the insatiable longing of a being wherein infinite ideals are fettered and cramped by a miserable actuality ; and so long as man is less than an angel and more than a beast, this cry will not for a moment fail to make itself heard.   Wonderfully uniform, too, is its tenor : in all ages, in all countries, in all creeds, whether it come from the Brahmin sage, the Persian poet, or the Christian quietist, it is in essence an enunciation more or less clear, more or less eloquent, of the aspiration of the soul to cease altogether from self and to be at one with God."

[1] E. G. Browne in *A Year among the Persians*.

Mysticism, therefore, is not to be regarded as a religion in itself, but rather as the most vital element in all true religions, rising up in revolt against cold formality and religious torpor. Nor is it a philosophical system, though it has its own doctrine of the scheme of things. It is to be described rather as an attitude of mind ; an innate tendency of the human soul, which seeks to transcend reason and to attain to a direct experience of God, and which believes that it is possible for the human soul to be united with Ultimate Reality, when "God ceases to be an object and becomes an experience." Mysticism has been defined as "the immediate feeling of the unity of the self with God—it is the religious life at its very heart and centre—it is the endeavour to fix the immediateness of the life in God as such—in this God-intoxication, in which the self and the world are alike forgotten, the subject knows himself to be in possession of the highest and fullest truth." [1]

The aim of the mystics, then, is to establish a conscious relation with the Absolute, in which they find the personal object of love. They desire to know, only that they may love, and their desire for union is founded neither on curiosity nor self-interest. That union which they seek is "the supernatural union of likeness, begotten of love, which is the union of the human will with the Divine. They seek to realise the unfelt natural presence of God in creation—by entering into a personal relationship with the concealed Presence which is the Source of being." [2] While religion in general separates the Divine from the

---

[1] Pfleiderer.
[2] A. B. Sharpe, *Mysticism : Its True Nature and Value*, p. 140.

human, Mysticism, going beyond religion, aspires to intimate union with the Divine, to a penetration of the Divine within the soul and to a disappearance of the individuality, with all its modes of acting, thinking and feeling, in the Divine substance.   The mystic seeks to pass out of all that is merely phenomenal, out of all lower forms of reality, to become Being itself.

On what do the mystics base their claim to be able to undertake this " tremendous journey towards the mysterious Isles of Fire, the Icelands of abstraction and of love " ?   Mysticism postulates certain articles of faith as the basis of its assumptions.

Firstly, it maintains that the soul can see and perceive, with that spiritual sense, of which St. Augustine speaks, which penetrates through the veils of matter and perceives the Light Unchangeable.   This is that inner sense which is called intuition, by means of which man can receive direct revelation and knowledge of God, by which he perceives things hidden from reason, through which he is brought into a conscious fellowship and unity with God.   " It is a spiritual sense opening inwardly, as the physical senses open outwardly, and because it has the capacity to perceive, grasp and know the truth at first hand, independent of all external sources of information, we call it intuition." [1]   All possibility of spiritual revelation depends upon such a spiritual faculty of the soul, capable of receiving it.   Mysticism, then, denies that knowledge can be attained only by means of the senses, or the intellect, or the normal processes of consciousness, and claims that the highest knowledge can be attained, and can only be attained, by this spiritual sense of intuition.

---

[1] R. W. Trine, *In Tune with the Infinite,* p. 40.

Secondly, Mysticism assumes that man must be a partaker of the Divine nature, if he is to know the Divine—only if the self is real can it hope to know Reality, and so it assumes that every creature is by nature akin to the Creator, there is within every living soul a divine spark, that which seeks re-union with the Eternal Flame. The mystics throughout the ages have contended that God Himself is " the ground of the soul " and that all men in the depths of their being have a share in one central, Divine, life. By the mystic, God is realised as " the foundation of the soul's being, and the soul's perception of its own essence is, in fact, the perception of its unity with the Divine nature."

In the third place, Mysticism assumes that none can attain to the knowledge of God except by purification from self. " Who shall ascend unto the hill of the Lord ? or who shall stand in His holy place ? Even he that hath clean hands and a pure heart," sang the Hebrew Psalmist, and the Greek philosopher Plotinus says also that as the eye could not behold the sun unless it were itself sunlike, so no more can the soul behold God unless it is Godlike. So the mystics both in East and West have maintained that the stripping from the soul of selfishness and sensuality is essential for the beholding of the Vision of God. Self-loss, withdrawal from self, self-annihilation, these are essential to those who would approach the Absolute. Only when all images of earth are hushed and the clamour of the senses is stilled and the soul has passed beyond thought of self can the Eternal Wisdom be revealed to the mystic who seeks that high communion with the Unseen.

Fourthly, the guide on the upward path of the

mystic is, and must be, Love.  The Oriental mystic, seeking to overcome the element ,of Not-Being—all that is opposed to the one Reality, the Divine Being Itself—finds that self, the great hindrance, can be conquered only by Love.  " By Love and Love alone can the dark shadow of Not-Being be done away : by Love and by Love alone can the soul of man win back to its Divine source and find its ultimate goal in reunion with the Truth." [1]  To the mystic, wherever he is found, and to whatever type of religion he attaches himself, the Object of his search is conceived of as the Beloved, and the mystic regards himself as the lover, yearning for the consummation of his love in union with the One he loves.  So the Flemish mystic Ruysbroeck writes : " When love has carried us above all things . . . we receive in peace the Incomprehensible Light " ; and again : " The God-seeking man who has forsaken self and all things . . . can always enter into the inmost part of his spirit.  There he feels himself to be an eternal life of love, which craves above all else to be one with God."  And from this we see that the term Love as used by the mystics implies far more than a mere emotion :  " it is to be understood in its deepest, fullest sense ; as the ultimate expression of the self's most vital tendencies . . . the deep-seated desire and tendency of the soul towards its source. . . . Love, to the mystic, is the active expression of his will and desire for the Absolute and also his innate tendency to that Absolute." [2]  Only Love can set the mystic free to pass from that which seems to that which is, to look upon the Light Unchangeable, to realise that

[1] E. J. W. Gibb, *History of Ottoman Poetry*, i, p. 20.
[2] E. Underhill, *Mysticism*, pp. 101 ff.

he is one with that Transcendental Ideal, where is the Supremely Real.

While Mysticism has thus developed a speculative system which has for its chief theory the fundamental unity, and the religious necessity of the union, of the Divine spirit with the human, it is also practical, issuing in a life to be lived by a rule, the Mystic Way, which must be trodden by those who seek to enjoy the blessedness of actual communion with the Highest.

The stages of the Mystic Way vary somewhat in the different religions of East and West in which Mysticism has taken root, but the threefold division which has been accepted in the West will, to a large extent, cover the stages of that Way as set forth in the religious systems of the East. These three stages are those of the Purgative life, the Illuminative life and the Unitive life, and the old Ṣūfī teacher who said that Renunciation, which is the keynote of the Way, should be first of that which is unlawful, second of that which is lawful, and third of all save God Himself, was describing the three stages of the Mystic Way fairly accurately.

At the beginning of all must be the awakening or the conversion of the mystic, who becomes aware of what he seeks, and sets his face towards the Goal. But a long preparation is needed before he can expect to attain it, and the discipline of the Purgative life must first be endured. By repentance, confession, amendment of life, must the self be disciplined. To the Eastern mystics, and to many mystics of the West, a life of asceticism has seemed the only way by which the carnal soul could be purified from its sins, which have their root in the desires of self, sensuality and

selfishness. For the mystic who lives in the world—
and the best of the mystics have not withdrawn
themselves from the business of life—this stage will
mean the full development of the civic and social
virtues and the discharge of all ordinary religious
duties and the use of the ordinary means of grace.
In this stage of the Way the soul seeks to be cleansed
from the senses, to be stripped of all that is opposed
to the Eternal Order and so to be fit to pass on to the
second stage, that of the Illuminative life.

The external life has been brought into accordance
with the Good and now the struggle is transferred
to the inner life. All the faculties, feeling, intellect
and will must be cleansed and brought into harmony
with the Eternal Will. This is the Ṣūfī doctrine of
unification : an old Persian writer says that it means
the cessation of human volition and affirmation of
the Divine Will, so as to exclude all personal initiative.
So also it is described by a modern writer as " the
complete surrender of man's personal striving to the
overruling Will of God and thus the linking up of all
the successive acts of life with the Abiding." [1] Now
is the soul walking in the light, looking upon a world
illuminated by the effulgence of Unclouded Light,
and the Presence of God is now an experienced reality,
not simply a concept of the imagination.

The final stage of the Way is the Unitive life, in
which the soul passes from Becoming to Being, man
beholds God face to face, and is joined to Him in a
progressive union, a union which is a fact of experience
consciously realised. In terms of the most beautiful
and glowing imagery have the mystics—who alone
are qualified to speak, since they alone have seen and

[1] E. Underhill, *Man and the Supernatural*, p. 246.

known that of which they speak—sought to describe
the Beatific Vision and the Union to which it leads.
Plotinus, who had seen and attained, speaks of it thus :
" Beholding this Being—resting, rapt, in the vision
and possession of so lofty a loveliness, growing to
Its likeness—what beauty can the soul yet lack ?   For
This, the Beauty supreme, the absolute and the
primal, fashions Its lovers to Beauty and makes them
also worthy of love." [1]

So also the Sūfī poet :

" With my Belovèd I alone have been,
  When secrets tenderer than evening airs
  Passed and the Vision blest
  Was granted to my prayers,
  That crowned me, else obscure, with endless fame,
  The while amazed between
  His Beauty and His Majesty
  I stood in silent ecstasy
  Revealing that which o'er my spirit went and came.
  Lo, in His face commingled
  Is every charm and grace ;
  The whole of Beauty singled
  Into a perfect face
  Beholding Him would cry,
  ' There is no God but He and He is the most High.' " [2]

We can set beside this the Franciscan concept of the
Vision as " a rapture and uplifting of the mind
intoxicated in the contemplation of the unspeakable
savour of the Divine sweetness, and a happy, peaceful
and sweet delight of the soul, that is rapt and uplifted
in great marvel—and a burning sense within of that
celestial glory unspeakable." [3]   Suso, the German

[1] Plotinus, *Ennead*, i. 7.
[2] Ibn al-Fārid, tr. R. A. Nicholson.
[3] *Little Flowers of St. Francis*, tr. T. W. Arnold, pp. 290, 291.

mystic of the fourteenth century, also seeks to give us a description of that which he finds words are too poor to depict : " This highest stage of union is an indescribable experience, in which all idea of images and forms and differences has vanished. All consciousness of self and of all things has gone and the soul is plunged into the abyss of the Godhead and the spirit has become one with God."

From the great Spanish mystic St. John of the Cross we have a similar testimony : " Thus the soul, when it shall have driven away from itself all that is contrary to the Divine Will, becomes transformed in God in love—the soul then becomes immediately enlightened by and transformed in God, because He communicates His own supernatural being in such a way that the soul seems to be God Himself and to possess the things of God—the soul seems to be God rather than itself and indeed is God by participation."

Mysticism, then, is spiritual and transcendent in its aims, but it holds that the Object of its quest, the World-Soul, the Absolute, the One Reality, is also the Beloved, and as lovers the mystics seek for union with the One.   That union they believe can be attained only by passing through certain definite stages, which they call the treading of the Mystic Way, so that Mysticism is active and practical ; it means discipline and a rule of life, and much upward striving before the mystic can hope to attain the heights.   Mysticism, since it is permeated through and through by the power of Love, can never be self-seeking, for the end can only be attained by self-stripping ; moreover, what is given in full measure to the mystic must be shared with others.   That flooding of the mystic's soul with the Divine Life must mean a fuller, richer life lived in contact with other human lives. " The perfect life," said Plato, " would be a life of perfect communion with other souls, as well as with the Soul which animates the universe." This mystic consciousness of the Presence of God is not given simply to delight in as the most exquisite of pleasures, but is to inspire the mystic to a finer service of humanity ; the purest Mysticism is found where the mystic " throws himself into action and life as though it were forever, and does it simply, without attempts to be isolated with the Absolute out of Time." So the active life of service in the world has been found necessary to the greatest of the mystics, who have felt themselves to be living in God, as in some measure deified in all their being and so in all their acts to be only instruments of God.

To sum up, then, in the words of a great modern teacher of Mysticism : " To be a mystic is simply to participate here and now in real and eternal life, in the fullest, deepest sense which is possible to man. It is to share as a free and conscious agent in the joyous travail of the universe, its mighty, onward sweep through pain and glory to its home in God. The ordered sequence of states, the organic development, whereby his consciousness is detached from illusion and rises to the mystic freedom which conditions, instead of being conditioned by, its normal world, is the way he must tread in order to attain. Only by this deliberate fostering of his deeper self, this transmutation of the elements of character, can he reach those levels of consciousness upon which he hears and responds to the measure " whereto the worlds keep time " on their great pilgrimage towards the Heart of God.  The mystic act of union, that joyous loss of the transfigured self in God, which is the crown of man's conscious ascent towards the Absolute, is the contribution of the individual to this, the destiny of the Cosmos." [1]

[1] E. Underhill, *Mysticism*, p. 534.

# CHAPTER II

# HEBREW AND JEWISH MYSTICISM

ALTHOUGH Judaism, with its deeply rooted conviction of the transcendence of God, its strong emphasis on legalism and formal ritual, and its narrow spirit of exclusiveness, might seem to provide a most un-promising environment for the growth and develop-ment of mysticism, yet, as we have noted, there is a mystical element in all true religions, and this is not lacking in Judaism.

It is evident that those men of God, prophets and seers and kings, whose experiences are set forth to us in the Old Testament were conscious of a close and personal communion with God, and were deeply convinced of His nearness to them and of His presence in the universe. To the Psalmist, all the beauties of the natural world were a revelation of the Divine, of the God " Who maketh the clouds His chariot, Who walketh upon the wings of the wind," [1] of Whom he asks, " Whither shall I go from Thy spirit ? or whither shall I flee from Thy presence ? " [2] He felt that Divine presence not only round about him but dwelling within himself also : " I am continually with Thee : Thou hast holden me by my right hand " [3]; and again he prays : " Cast me not away from Thy presence and take not Thy holy spirit from me." [4]

We find the same consciousness of communion with God among the prophets. Isaiah's vision in the temple was typical of the experience of the mystics of all ages, when he saw a God " Whose train filled the temple," emblematic of the all-inclusive, penetrating

[1] Ps. civ. 3.       [2] Ps. cxxxix. 7.
[3] Ps. lxxiii. 23.       [4] Ps. li. 11.

presence of the Most High, and when, having been purified by the cleansing power of the Divine Love, he consecrated himself in complete self-surrender to the Will of God. Both in the prophet Jeremiah and perhaps in the Canticles we find the relation of God and the soul symbolised by the mystic image of lover and beloved. " I have loved thee with an everlasting love : therefore with loving-kindness have I drawn thee," [1] says the Divine Lover. " My beloved is mine and I am His," [2] says the soul rejoicing in union with the God she loves.

Ezekiel and the Apocalyptic writers had without a doubt passed through the experience of the mystic ecstasy and the knowledge of things Divine to which it led them, and in the Enoch literature there is much mystic lore. The gift of prophecy itself indicated that certain men had a spiritual endowment not possessed by mankind in general, which enabled them to attain to the knowledge of God, and to receive, as the result of a direct immediate experience, that which He had to reveal to them. This was akin to the " gnosis " of later times, the intuitive knowledge of God granted only to the mystic.

Two distinct schools of Jewish mystical thought are to be found : the Rabbinic or Talmudic Midrashic school, which had its rise in Palestine and later developed into the Qabbalah of the Middle Ages ; and the Jewish-Hellenistic school, which originated in Alexandria, and which also had considerable influence upon later Jewish mystical thought. We find too that among the Jews, as elsewhere, Mysticism was associated with asceticism and withdrawal from the world, as exemplified in the sects of the Essenes and Therapeutæ.

[1] Jer. xxxi. 3.  [2] Cant. ii. 16.

The Rabbinic school of Jewish mysticism, as we might expect, concerned itself mainly with the Old Testament, though as time went on, foreign elements became incorporated. An essentially Jewish conception was that of the " Shekinah," the Presence or manifestation of God dwelling among men. This was developed from the Old Testament conception of God as Father and as King, a conception which involved a close and loving relationship between God and man, and yet a constant realisation of the Divine majesty, and this was summed up by the term " Shekinah," which is literally a " dwelling " of God with His creatures. It was an emanation embodying the Divine Presence, and though always present, it could be realised by the individual only after spiritual and moral discipline ; the mystic must tread the way of purgation before he could hope to attain to the knowledge of God. Of the chariot of Solomon, " the midst thereof being paved with love," [1] the Rabbis said that the love in the midst thereof was the Shekinah, the chariot being the Universe, which is pervaded throughout by the Presence of God, and reveals in all its parts that indwelling of the Divine Love.

This school of Jewish mysticism gave much attention to the mystical interpretation of the first chapter of Genesis and the Vision of Ezekiel, and the latter gave rise to the " Merkabah " or Chariot conception, this being the term applied to the vision as a whole. The Merkabah or Chariot represented the Mystic Way, by which the mystic, designated as the Merkabah-traveller, might be enabled, while still in the flesh, to ascend to the spiritual heights. The vision

[1] Cant. iii. 10.

typified the longing of the human soul for the sight
of the Divine Presence and companionship with It,
and the image of the glory of the Lord was interpreted
as a Divine self-opening to men, the soul being urged
to union with God because of its feeling that God has
first gone out to seek union with it. But knowledge
of this mystic Merkabah lore was to be allowed only
to the initiated, who were fitted to receive it.[1]

The mystical treatise *Sēfer Yesīrā*, which may
have originated as early as the second century B.C.,
though parts of it suggest a later date, elaborates these
elements of the Rabbinic school. It represents a
mystical philosophy derived from the forms and
values of the letters of the Hebrew alphabet, and in this,
as in other respects, shews kinship with the mediæval
Qabbalah. It develops a doctrine of emanation, all
existing things being regarded as successive outflowings
of God, Who is not external to anything in His universe:
everything originally was comprehended in Him, and
all multiplicity is but an emanation of the one Unity,
a manifestation of the God from Whom all came
and to Whom all must return, because they are
ultimately one with the One, as the flame is one with
the candle whence it comes forth.

The book describes the " Ten Sefīrōt," or spiritual
agencies, which emanate from God, and which are the
spirit, air, water, fire, the four cardinal points of the
compass, height and depth. All things emanate from
the first of the Sefīrōt, that is, the Spirit of the Living
God. All things therefore have their origin in God,
yet the author is careful to guard himself against
pantheism, for he says, " The last of the Sefīrōt unites
itself to its first just as a flame is united with the candle,

[1] Cf. J. Abelson, *Jewish Mysticism*, chap. ii.

for God is one and there is no second." So the book of the *Yesīrā* teaches that God and the world are a unity, but though God is immanent, He is also transcendent.

Of greater importance than the *Sēfer Yesīrā* as a text-book of Jewish mysticism is the *Zohar* (lit. Shining, or Brightness), which made its appearance in Spain in the thirteenth century A.D., but which in part probably goes back to the second century, though it is obviously not the work of a single author or of one period only. The *Zohar* purports to be a commentary on the Pentateuch, but actually is a manual of mystic theosophy ; it makes plain that the essence of the Torah is its mystical sense, and by an understanding of this mystical sense and a life led in accordance with it, man can ascend to God. The world being a series of emanations from the Divine, and the outward expression of the Thought of God, man can everywhere behold the image of God, and by leading the " good life " he can make his way to the Invisible Author of all he sees, the Cause of causes, and so come to have union with the Unseen.

The world is considered to be made up of four component parts—the world of emanation, the world of creative ideas, the world of creative formation and the world of creative matter. The manifestation of the Divine Will is to be found in all these parts, hence Evil is outside of them, an illusion, non-existent. The conception of the " Ten Sefīrōt " appears again, as the One manifesting Himself in plurality, and the Crown of them is the Heavenly Man, the Primal Adam, through whom earthly man was created. Here we find the distinction between the Godhead and God in action, and it is bound up with the doctrine of the

Divine Name, with which Rabbinic mysticism was closely concerned.  According to the *Zohar*, " I am that I am " represents the unmanifested Godhead, the Absolute containing in Himself the All, the " Ĕn-Sōf " (= Endless, Infinite) ; while " Jahweh " denotes the Divine self-manifestation, God as immanent in the cosmos.

The *Zohar* describes the relation of the soul to the body as being that of God to the world ; the soul is an emanation from the Oversoul of the universe, and it was with sorrow that it obeyed the command of God to take its way to earth.  The soul includes the rational element—which links it with the Divine—the moral, and the physical—which holds it to the earth— and here, perhaps, we have a Platonic element in the *Zohar*, which elsewhere shews the influence of Neo-Platonism.  As in nearly all systems of Mysticism, Love leads the soul on its upward way.  It seeks to enter consciously into the presence of God, but it can do so only under the urge of ecstatic love.  This ecstatic love can be realised in this life: " Whoso serves God out of love comes into union with the place of the Highest of the High, and comes into union, too, with the holiness of the world which is to be."  When the soul has completed the cycle of its earthly career and hastens back to be united with the Oversoul, it finds its deepest satisfaction in the ecstasies of love, which it can taste but briefly in this life.  " There is in heaven," says the writer, " a hidden palace called the Palace of Love.  There are gathered together all the souls beloved of the Heavenly King ; it is there that the Heavenly King dwells with these holy souls and unites Himself to them by kisses of love." [1]

[1] *Zohar* ii. 97.

Since mystics have always found that asceticism and withdrawal from the world, either temporary or permanent, have been the means to their end, it is not surprising that among the Jews also we find the tendency to form orders of recluses devoted to mystic contemplation, the most famous of whom were the Essenes and the Therapeutæ. The Jewish historian Josephus gives us a full account of the Essenes, and Philo has much to say of them and other Jewish recluses. The date at which they first made their appearance is uncertain, but they appear to have been in existence from about 150 B.C. up to the Fall of Jerusalem. They were a society of devotees who at first were to be found chiefly in the country to the west of the Dead Sea, where they sought in solitude a refuge from the evils of the world. Later they formed colonies in other parts of Palestine, and Josephus estimates their numbers at four thousand. They were practical mystics and yet had a certain speculative mysticism of their own. They gave up most of their time to the practice of husbandry, and with this aimed at a life of true virtue. Pleasures, says Josephus, they rejected as an evil, and continence and the conquest over their passions as virtue. They practised celibacy, but took young children to train in their manner of life. They despised riches and had all things in common ; they taught absolute obedience to their directors, and silence was the rule within their dwellings. There was a preliminary novitiate of a year and then a period of two years' probation before they took the solemn vows of the order and were sworn to secrecy as to their doctrines. Like the Stoics, the Essenes despised the miseries of life, and proved themselves, in time of persecution, able to rise above physical pain, for they believed that while their bodies were corruptible their souls were immortal. Says Josephus: " They believe that their souls continue for ever and come out of the most subtle air and are united to their bodies as to prisons, into which they are drawn by a certain natural enticement, but that when they are set free from the bonds of the flesh, they then, as released from a long bondage, rejoice and mount upward." [1]

The Essenes, then, were an order of Jewish monks who combined the contemplative with the practical life, believing it right to occupy the senses and provide for their own needs, while not neglecting the practice of devoted contemplation.

The Therapeutæ were also an order of recluses existing in Egypt about the end of the first century B.C. and the opening of the first century A.D., and they are described by Philo in his treatise " Concerning the Contemplative Life." Eusebius, quoting from Philo,[2] tries to claim the Therapeutæ as Christian ascetics, but it is obvious from Philo's description that they were Jews. They were to be found near Alexandria and especially near Lake Mareotis. Their name was derived from their being physicians of souls, or from their pure and sincere service of God. They lived in groups of huts, like the " lauræ " of the later Christian monks of Egypt and Syria, having effected a complete renunciation of and withdrawal from the world in order to attain in ecstasy to the highest vision of God and the truth. At sunrise, says Philo, they prayed for a day of true happiness, that their minds might receive the Divine illumination, and at sunset they prayed that their soul, freed from sensuality, might in turning

[1] Josephus, *Wars*, ii. 8. 2–10.    [2] *Eccles. Hist.* ii. 17.

inwards search out Truth. They practised celibacy
and asceticism in moderation, and their numbers
included women as well as men. Unlike the Essenes,
the Therapeutæ limited themselves to the contemplative life, for " they," says Philo, " live wholly for the
contemplation of the reality of things, and of the soul,
citizens of Heaven as well as of earth, friends, through
their virtue, of the Father and Creator of the world." [1]

In the Jewish-Hellenistic school of mysticism, the
theology of Judaism was studied in conjunction with the
writings of Plato and Aristotle. Typical of this
school of thought is the *Book of the Wisdom of Solomon*, written by an Egyptian Jew of the last century
before Christ. It gives an account of the way of
thought and life of the righteous, an exhortation to
seek wisdom, and a description of the work of the
Divine Wisdom in history. Wisdom is here personified, and is endowed with the attributes of the Stoic
Logos. " Wisdom," says the writer, " is the worker
of all things, a spirit, understanding, holy, one only,
manifold, subtle, lively, clear, undefiled—penetrating
all understanding, pure and subtle spirits. She is the
breath of the power of God and a pure influence flowing
from the glory of the Almighty. She is the brightness
of the everlasting light, the unspotted mirror of the
power of God and the image of His goodness—in all
ages entering into holy souls, she maketh them friends
of God and prophets." [2] Wisdom is here depicted
as an independent spiritual being acting alongside of
God, as His mediator in regard to the creation, preser-
vation and ruling of the world. Wisdom leads those
who love her unto the incorruption which is im-

[1] Cf. O. Pfleiderer, *Primitive Christianity*, iii, chap. i.
[2] *Wisdom of Solomon*, vii. 22–27.

mortality. " I pondered," says the writer, " how that
to be allied unto Wisdom is immortality " ; and again :
" For to know Thee is perfect righteousness : yea, to
know Thy power is the root of immortality." [1]   It was
to this end that God created man, to this end that He
manifests Himself in all things : " Thou lovest all the
things that are, and abhorrest nothing which Thou
hast made.—But Thou sparest all : for they are
Thine, O Lord, Thou Lover of souls. For Thine
incorruptible Spirit is in all things." [2]   To this writer
God and His universe are a unity, and because of the
Divine within him man can attain to communion with,
can return unto, the Source whence he came.

As we have already seen, Jewish mysticism felt the
need for a mediator between God and man, to bridge
the gulf between the transcendent Godhead and the
world in which God manifests Himself as immanent.
So we have the conception of the Logos, personified in
some measure as the Divine Wisdom in this *Book of
Wisdom*, a conception developed and completed by
Philo (born about 20 B.C.), in whom the combination of
Greek philosophy with the revealed religion of the Old
Testament may be said to have reached its consummation.

Philo makes a clear distinction between God Who is
pure Being, unknowable, exalted above the world,
incomparable, and God revealed, Who is immanent
in man and the universe, all-penetrating, and all-
filling. Though God is the One and the All, He is
not to be identified with His world, so Philo makes
use of " Logoi," divine agencies to act between God
and the world, who manifest the energy of God, and
give creation all its reality and order and beauty.   The

---

[1] *Wisdom of Solomon,* xii. 1.         [2] *Ibid.,* xi. 24 ff.

chief of these powers is the Logos, Who is the Beginning, the Word and the Image of God, and Who is
man's chief helper in his striving towards the Divine.
Man is earthly as regards his body, but by his intelligence he is related to the Divine, of which he is an
emanation and a reflection. Philo distinguishes between those who come to a knowledge of God through
His creation and those who have attained to the
knowledge of Him in His immediate self-manifestation, who love God for His own sake ; only those who
have attained to this knowledge and this love are the
true sons of God.[1] By contemplation and in solitude
can man realise his oneness with the Divine, can learn
how to follow God and become like Him. Love must
be the basis of all true virtue—love to God displayed
in joyous devotion, and love to man shewn in service.
Those who practise such virtue are the friends of God,
partakers in His power, even in a sense themselves
gods.

There are three stages on the Mystic Way : first,
asceticism, which means strife with the lower passions ;
then knowledge, which means not only conquering the
senses, but going out of the self into ecstasy, when
the soul drinks deeply of heavenly love and is drawn
upwards to God. Here we have the familiar stages
of Purgation and Illumination. The third stage is
the unitive life, when the God-given nature becomes a
partaker of the royal virtue, receiving the perfect gifts
of God and abiding in them. To those who have
been thus perfected is granted the vision of God in
mystical ecstasy, but it is only granted when the soul
withdraws itself from all finite things and even transcends itself, as Philo tells us ; when the mind, laid

[1] Cf. A. Neander, *Church History,* i, p. 78.

hold of by the Divine Love, penetrates in its ardour into the Holy of Holies it forgets itself and all else in the passionate joy of losing its own consciousness within the Divine Light of God. This vision is the object of the mystic's quest, and at the last his striving is rewarded. " What lovelier or more fitting garland could be woven for the victorious soul than the power, with clear vision, to gaze upon Him Who is ? Truly splendid is the prize held out to the wrestling soul— to be equipped with eyesight so as to perceive without dimness Him Who is alone worthy of contemplation."

To Philo, the search for the mystic vision of the Divine is in the highest degree the service of God, but it is not to be separated from the service of man. The contemplative life must be combined with the active life of the practical mystic. " Both the exclusive lovers of man," he says, " and the exclusive lovers of God we may rightly call half-perfect in virtue. The perfectly virtuous are those who excel in both." [1] Here Philo foreshadows the teaching of the greatest of the mystics who were to come after him ; the perfect man must live the " universal life," lived Godwards and manwards.

To Philo, though his mysticism was drawn from Rabbinic as well as Hellenic sources, Christian mysticism has been much indebted, and his influence was also evident in the later developments of Jewish mysticism, especially the teaching of the two great mystic theologians of the Middle Ages, Solomon b. Gabirol (c. 1021–1051) and Abraham b. Ezra (1092–1167), who cannot be dealt with here.

[1] Cf. I. Abrahams, *Some Permanent Values in Judaism,* chap. iii.

# CHAPTER III

# MYSTICISM IN THE NEW TESTAMENT

As we have seen, there is a mystical element in the Old Testament, appearing here and there : in the New Testament we find a fully developed mysticism, set forth most plainly in the Pauline and Johannine writings.

St. Paul was himself a mystic, and possessed of a temperament susceptible to the influences which he found around him—the philosophy of the Greeks, the teachings of the later Jewish scriptures, and the writings of his co-religionist Philo, all strongly tinged with mysticism.  His was a nature to which religion made an irresistible appeal ;  for him God was all in all, and his soul craved for a relationship with the Divine, which should bring him into the closest communion and intimacy with the God he worshipped. His life, as we know it, shews clearly the stages by which he attained to the mystic's aim, the unitive life lived in constant fellowship with the Divine.  He knew what he sought even before his conversion, but it was the vision on the road to Damascus which shewed him the way, and made him realise that communion with God was to be attained through Christ, God manifested to man.  After his conversion, he had still a long way to go before he could attain to what he sought, and he went immediately into retreat, and during those years in Arabia passed through the stage of the Purgative life, which meant the conquest of his carnal self, and then, when he was prepared for what God had to reveal to him, he knew what it was to be rapt away into ecstasy, caught up beyond time and space, to behold the immediate vision of Reality,[1]

[1] 2 Cor. xii. 2–4 ;  Ephes. iii. 3.

and thenceforward he entered upon the illuminative life, walking in the light. Yet there were many years still to be passed before at last he attained to the unitive life, when he was continually conscious of the indwelling Divine Presence, and could say, " I live, yet not I, but Christ liveth in me " [1] ; and again, " The law of the Spirit of life in Christ Jesus hath made me free from the law of sin and death." [2] This constant sense of the Divine Presence within him was a source of increasing spiritual strength and power to him in his work. " I can do all things," he writes from his prison, " through Christ which strengtheneth me." [3] It was his own first-hand experience that enabled St. Paul to write so confidently to his converts and to the young Christian Churches of the way whereby salvation might be attained.

St. Paul was not only a mystic himself but a teacher of mystical doctrine, and while his own experience was the basis of his teaching, the form in which he clothed it shews how much he was affected by Alexandrian Hellenism. It is plain that he was thoroughly acquainted with the *Book of the Wisdom of Solomon* referred to in our last chapter. Phrase after phrase which he uses finds its parallel there. " The fruit of the Spirit is love," writes St. Paul. [4] " Wisdom is a loving spirit," writes the author of the *Book of Wisdom*, [5] who says also, " Love is the keeping of her laws," [6] which is found in St. Paul as " Love is the fulfilling of the law." [7] Again St. Paul writes : " I am carnal, sold under sin.—Know ye not that your body is the temple of the Holy Ghost ? " [8] which re-echoes the

---

[1] Gal. ii. 20.    [2] Rom. viii. 2.    [3] Phil. iv. 13.
[4] Gal. v. 22.    [5] i. 6.    [6] vi. 18.
[7] Rom. xiii. 10.         [8] Rom. vii. 14 ; 1 Cor. vi. 19.

statement of the earlier writer, " Wisdom shall not dwell in the body that is subject unto sin." [1]   In the epistles to the Ephesians and Colossians, where the author speaks of Christ as " the image of the invisible God, the first-born of every creature : For by Him were all things created, that are in heaven, and that are in earth, visible and invisible, whether they be thrones, or dominions, or principalities, or powers : all things were created by Him, and for Him : And He is before all things, and by Him all things consist," [2] we find signs of the Philonic conception of the Logos as the mediator of the invisible in His relation to the world, a mediator Who is the first-born Son of God.   The same idea, found also in the Gnostics, is contained in the verse, " For in Him dwelleth all the fullness of the Godhead bodily." [3]

St. Paul, in his teachings, shews plainly his conviction that man is a partaker of the Divine nature, a conviction which is at the root of all mysticism, and it is this affinity which makes the finite human spirit capable of being filled with the Divine Spirit.   Man is " the image and glory of God " ;   God is not far from every one of us, " For in Him we live and move and have our being." [4]   Again he writes : " Of Him, and through Him, and to Him, are all things : to Whom be glory for ever." [5]   We have the witness to this kinship with the Divine within ourselves : " The Spirit itself beareth witness with our spirit, that we are the children of God.—One God and Father of all, Who is above all, and through all, and in you all." [6]

The conditions on which man can ascend the upward way and attain to the unitive life with and in God are

---

[1] *Book of Wisdom*, i. 4.     [2] Col. i. 15–17.     [3] Col. ii. 9.
[4] Acts xvii. 27–28.   [5] Rom. xi. 36.   [6] Rom. viii. 16 ; Ephes. iv. 6.

to St. Paul those which we find in nearly all doctrines of the Mystic Way. There must be a cleansing from all defilement both of the flesh and of the spirit. " Having therefore these promises, dearly beloved," says St. Paul, pointing upward to the heights, " let us cleanse ourselves from all filthiness of the flesh and spirit, perfecting holiness in the fear of God." [1] Only those who have purified themselves as He is pure can hope to see God, but the evil tendencies of the flesh can be neutralised by the power of the spirit. " To be carnally minded is death," the apostle warns those to whom he writes ; " but to be spiritually minded is life and peace.—For if ye live after the flesh, ye shall die : but if ye through the Spirit do mortify the deeds of the body, ye shall live." [2] He urges those who have learned from the example of Christ how to live in this world to follow in the steps of their Master and set their affections on things above and not on things of the earth. Let them put off the " old man," with the lusts thereof, which belong to the life apart from God, and be renewed and put on the " new man," and so become that which God meant them to be, which He created them to be, in righteousness and true holiness. St. Paul would have the individual Christian relive the life of Christ and personally experience that same redemptive process, which would mean not only sharing in His sufferings, the " crucifying " of the carnal self, but rising again with Him to a new birth, the life lived in God. " Be ye transformed," he says, " by the renewing of your mind, that ye may prove what is that good, and acceptable, and perfect, will of God." [3] By the gift of the Spirit, the inner life is transformed, so that it becomes assimilated to the

[1] 2 Cor. vii. 1.    [2] Rom. viii. 6, 13.    [3] Rom. xii. 2.

Divine life. " He that is joined unto the Lord is one spirit." [1]

Not self-mastery and enlightenment alone, but love is a necessary accompaniment of faith on the upward way, and we need not dwell here on St. Paul's great Hymn of Love,[2] love as shewn by man towards man, the image of God. But the love of man for God is even more indestructible and reaches to yet greater heights.[3] By love of God alone can man hope to attain to knowledge of Him, and to that life of communion which is and must be " rooted and grounded in love." Only so can man be perfected and attain unto the stature of the fullness of Christ, and so become like unto God.

To those who have attained is granted the vision of God as He is ; a vision not granted to the finite, human understanding, but only to be spiritually discerned by those fitted to receive it. " Eye hath not seen, nor ear heard, neither have entered into the heart of man, the things which God hath prepared for them that love Him. But God hath revealed them unto us by His Spirit." [4] Those who are still imperfect, children in the Mystic Way, can know and see but imperfectly, but from those who are perfected nothing is withheld. " Now we see through a glass, darkly ; but then face to face : now I know in part ; but then shall I know even as also I am known." [5]

Those who have known and seen are become the children of God, in whom and with whom He dwells, and through whom He works. Their life is lived henceforth in conscious union with Him. " As many as are led by the Spirit of God, they are the

---

[1] 1 Cor. vi. 17.          [2] 1 Cor. xiii.          [3] Rom. viii. 35–39.
[4] 1 Cor. ii. 9–10.                        [5] 1 Cor. xiii. 12.

sons of God." [1]   And in the most beautiful of all the
mystic images which he uses, St. Paul shews how
those who gaze upon the Divine Beauty themselves
become Godlike.   " We all, with open face beholding
as in a glass the glory of the Lord, are changed into
the same image from glory to glory, even as by the
Spirit of the Lord." [2]   God has granted this vision,
as He has given Himself in union to those who love
Him, for the carrying out of His Divine Will, that they
may be " filled with all the fullness of God," and so
through His union with them, He may work in them
" both to will and to do of His good pleasure."   Here
and now man can attain unto immortality, sharing in
the Divine Life and the Divine Work, God and man
one in the fulfilment of the Everlasting Purpose.

St. John does not give us any account of his own
spiritual experiences, and we have no evidence that
he was himself a mystic, though he must have had
a profound understanding of, and sympathy with,
the mystical teaching which he sets forth in his books.
He is primarily a theologian, and there is evidence
in his writings that his theology has been influenced
by both Plato and Philo.   His Gospel has been called
the " charter of Christian Mysticism," and he has made
all Christians familiar with the principles of mystical
religion.

To him God is Light and Love and Spirit, but since
the Absolute Godhead can be manifested only through
God revealed, the Incarnation is for St. John the
central fact of the Christian faith.   The doctrine of
the Logos, derived from the teaching of the Essenes
and Philo, he applies to Christ, God manifested in
the world, and this is St. John's own interpretation

[1] Rom. viii. 14.                    [2] 2 Cor. iii. 18.

of the Incarnation, for our Lord does not apply the term to Himself. " In the beginning was the Word," says St. John, " and the Word was with God and the Word was God. The same was in the beginning with God. All things were made by Him ; and without Him was not anything made that was made." [1] The Word, then, was God in action, the centre of all Life and Being, the Mind and the Wisdom (for St. John's Logos can be identified with the Divine Wisdom of the *Book of Wisdom*) which dominates and animates the whole universe. To St. John there are two worlds, the lower world of darkness and illusion and the world above of light and goodness, which alone is real. That man might be freed from unreality and sin, the Light shone here in the darkness, to guide men to that realm above, and so the Word is the Light of Light, lighting every man that cometh into the world.

Throughout his Gospel St. John emphasises not so much the outward life of Christ as His teaching, and to him religion is firstly and essentially an inward process of growth, depending upon direct experience. The end is Eternal Life, the life of God dwelling within the human spirit to which it has been imparted, the way thereto is by rebirth, and the Guide on the way is Christ, Himself both Revealer and Revealed, Enlightener and Light. Man himself is of Divine origin, and the Incarnation emphasises the bond, since for love of His children here in this world God sent forth His Son, that the darkness should not prevail, man should not perish, but through the Word should come into possession of everlasting life. " We know that we are of God," writes St. John, " and we

[1] John i. 1–3.

know that the Son of God is come, and hath given us an understanding, that we may know Him that is true, and we are in Him that is true, even in His Son Jesus Christ. This is the true God, and Eternal life." [1]

The Mystic Way, for St. John, includes a new birth and a purification from the old in order to enter into the new life. " Except a man be born again, he cannot see the kingdom of God.—Except a man be born of water and of the Spirit, he cannot enter into the kingdom of God. That which is born of the flesh is flesh ; and that which is born of the Spirit is spirit." [2]  It is the way of Purgation again—the carnal self must die, that the spiritual self may come to life. " It is the Spirit that quickeneth ; the flesh profiteth nothing." [3]  Complete renunciation of the world of darkness and unreality is necessary for those who would walk in the Light. " Except a corn of wheat fall into the ground and die, it abideth alone : but if it die, it bringeth forth much fruit. He that loveth his life shall lose it ; and he that hateth his life in this world shall keep it unto life eternal." [4]  Faith, then, shews itself in self-sacrifice and self-dedication, and with faith is joined love, and this is the main theme of St. John's first epistle, love to God and love to man. " Beloved," says the old man to his children in Christ, " let us love one another : for love is of God ; and every one that loveth is born of God, and knoweth God. He that loveth not knoweth not God ; for God is Love." [5]

To those who have died to self, and who in faith and love are seeking to do God's will, He grants the

[1] 1 John v. 19, 20.     [2] John iii. 3, 5, 6.     [3] John vi. 63.
[4] John xii. 24, 25.     [5] 1 John iv. 7, 8.

mystic union, whereby they partake of His Divine Life and abide in Him. " If that which ye have heard from the beginning shall remain in you, ye also shall continue in the Son, and in the Father." [1] " If a man love Me," says Christ, " he will keep My words : and we will come unto him, and make our abode with him." [2]   And again He says, in still more significant words : " He that eateth My flesh and drinketh My blood, dwelleth in Me, and I in him." [3]   This unitive life, lived in God through Christ, means an ever-present sense of the power of the Divine spirit working within. " Hereby know we that we dwell in Him, and He in us, because He hath given us of His Spirit." [4]   It means the satisfaction of all the desires of the soul, and life which is ever renewed. " He that cometh to Me shall never hunger ; and he that believeth on Me shall never thirst—the water that I shall give him shall be in him a well of water springing up into everlasting life." [5]

This, to St. John, was the whole purpose of the Incarnation ; God had manifested Himself to men that they might have life and might have it more abundantly, that here, in this present time, they might enter into the possession of Eternal Life.

[1] I John ii. 24.     [2] John xiv. 23.     [3] John vi. 56.
[4] I John iv. 13.     [5] John vi. 35 ; iv. 14.

CHAPTER IV

# MYSTICISM IN CLASSICAL TIMES

Since we take the word " Mysticism " from the
Greeks, among whom religious " mysteries " were
celebrated from an early period, it is perhaps not
surprising that we find a mystical element in nearly
all Greek philosophy.

The Orphics of the sixth century B.C. maintained a
mystical-speculative theory of religion. They held
that the soul was divine in its origin and therefore
naturally pure, and that the body was its tomb. To
this they joined the doctrine that only by a system of
purification, inward and outward, effected during a
series of lives, could the soul be released from the fetters
of the material and the sensual, and in the end attain to
mystic union with God, and so again become divine.

The Pythagoreans, of the same period, had much
in common with the Orphics, and were responsible
for the ethico-mystical doctrine of the transmigration
of souls. Purification with them took the form of
ascetic discipline and otherworldliness. They, too,
held that the soul was immortal, that is, it had something of the Divine within it, and the body was but
its temporary prison. The end of man was to become
like God.

The poet Pindar, who lived from about 522 B.C.
to 448 B.C., also expresses his belief that the soul is
divine in origin and has within it the possibility of
freeing itself from the trammels of the flesh by its
own efforts towards purity, and in his beautiful odes
he makes clear his belief in the immortality of the
soul, of which men can see signs even in this life, as
he writes in one of his songs :

" What are we ? what not ? things in one day ending !
Man is a dream through shadows dimly seen.
But when a glory shines from God descending
Then rests on men a sunbright splendour-sheen
And life serene." [1]

Plato (427–347 B.C.), though he must be regarded as the first great exponent of speculative mysticism, derives something from these earlier thinkers and most of all from his own master Socrates. Socrates was a seer as well as a philosopher, and throughout his life he felt himself to be in touch with the Divine. He was convinced of the reality of the human soul, of its kinship with the Divine and its consequent immortality. Plato, building on the foundations of his predecessors, holds that the soul, being of divine origin, has the instinctive longing to be at one with the eternal Being in the world, and this instinctive longing and the power to recognise and apprehend true Reality is derived from the soul's life before its birth into the temporary world, when it dwelt in the presence of pure Being and there contemplated eternal and unchanging Reality.

" Every soul," he says in the *Phædrus*, " has beheld true being, but few only retain an adequate remembrance of the holy things which once they saw. There was a time when they saw Beauty shining in brightness—shining in company with the celestial forms ; and coming to earth we find her here too, shining in clearness. He whose initiation is recent, and who has been a spectator of many glories in the other world, is amazed when he sees anyone having a godlike face or form, which is the expression of divine beauty, and again the old awe steals over him." [2]

---

[1] " To Aristomenes," tr. A. S. Way.     [2] Tr. Jowett.

The soul, then, in a previous existence, when she was regardless of what we now call being, raised up her head towards the true Being and beheld the vision of absolute Truth, and all her after-existence should be spent in regaining this. Once and again, to encourage her, she may have glimpses of the flashing beauty of That which she seeks, but only when the animal instincts have been subdued can that Vision be finally enjoyed. The one who employs his memories aright, and uses Reason to subjugate Passion, will be initiated into those great mysteries, and he alone can become truly perfect.

In the *Republic* Plato shews how true education should lead the soul to turn away its " eye," the spiritual sense, from the darkness in which it was born, towards the Sun of truth with which it is really akin. As the soul progresses in its knowledge of the spiritual, a new light is shed upon the natural world, and at last the soul is enabled to look upon the Good itself, not merely upon its reflections in the phenomenal world, but in its own dwelling-place, and in its Essence, and so to see that all things beautiful, in this visible world, or in that invisible one, are derived from this, the absolute Beauty.

With Plato also, as with all the mystics, the guide on the way of progress is Love. " Through love," he says in the *Symposium*, " all the intercourse and converse of God with man is carried on." By love the desire of the soul is raised from earthly to heavenly things. From love of one beautiful form the soul will pass to love of all beautiful forms and thence to love of wisdom, the true Beauty, and in a famous passage he describes the end and the reward of this love, speaking through the mouth of the wise woman Dio-

tima of Mantineia. " He who has been instructed
thus far in the things of love and who has learned to see
the beautiful in due order and succession, when he
comes towards the end will suddenly perceive a nature
of wondrous beauty, which is everlasting, not growing
and decaying, or waxing and waning, but Beauty
absolute, separate, simple and everlasting, which
without any change is imparted to the ever-growing
and perishing beauties of all other things. He who,
from these ascending, under the influence of true love,
begins to perceive that Beauty, is not far from the end.
And the true order of going, or being led by another,
to the things of love is to begin from the beauties of
earth and mount upwards for the sake of that other
Beauty, using these as steps only, going from fair forms
to fair practices and from fair practices to fair notions,
until from fair notions he arrives at the notion of
absolute Beauty and at last knows what the essence
of beauty is. This is that life above all others which
a man should live, in the contemplation of Beauty
absolute. . . . What if man had eyes to see the
true beauty, the Divine Beauty, pure and clear and
unalloyed, not clogged with the pollutions of mortality
and all the colours and vanities of human life, thither
looking and holding converse with the true beauty,
simple and divine ? Remember how in that communion only, beholding Beauty with the eye of the mind,
he will be enabled to bring forth, not the images of
beauty but realities—and bringing forth and nourish-
ing true virtue, to become the friend of God and be
immortal, if mortal man may." [1]

Plato, then, maintains those truths on which all
mystics base their faith. He implies that there is

[1] *Symposium,* tr. Jowett.

something in the nature of the soul which enables it to see that this world is a reflection of the truly Real, to recognise the eternal in the temporal and to rise through the sight of the seen to the perception of the unseen, that is to say, the soul has in itself an eye for divine Reality and is capable of attaining to the beatific vision. As we have seen, he holds that this capacity is due to the divine origin of the soul, which came from God and seeks to return to God, because of its kinship with the Absolute and Real and Eternal. The way to attain is by purification from the bodily and the sensual. " When none of the senses harass the soul," he says in the *Phædo*, " when she has dismissed the body and released herself as far as she can from all intercourse or contact with it and so coming to be alone with herself strives after real truth—that one will attain the knowledge of real Being, if any will." So, made pure by self-stripping and led on by love, the soul will attain in ecstasy to the contemplation of the Divine Beauty, and growing into that likeness will once more find its home in God.

Aristotle, though he was concerned mainly with the scientific classification of the phenomenal world, had a considerable influence upon Mysticism and succeeding mystics. God, to him, was the Absolutely Real, living, perfect, eternal, moveless Energy. But, though He is separated from the world, yet the firmament which He sets in motion does share in the Divinity with which the whole of Nature is invested. With Aristotle, as with Plato, the impulse of the soul is to be at one with the eternal Being in the world, and the only way open from man to God is the way of pure contemplation, in which, to Aristotle, beatitude consists. By pure contemplation it is possible to pass beyond what is accidental and transitory, beyond the limitations of time and space and at last to contemplate the Absolute. Man possesses an " active reason " which is divine in origin, is indeed one with the Divine Reason, and in contemplation the soul is one with that which it beholds, in a perfect unity.

The Stoic philosophy, which had its rise in the fifth century B.C., found a basis for unity in the doctrine of a Spirit immanent in the world and in man. The Divine Word or Reason was the vital principle whence all things came and by which all lived. Thus the soul of the individual partook of the nature of God and man had Divinity within him. So Cleanthes (331–251 B.C.) wrote in his great Hymn :

> " O God most glorious, called by many a name,
>   Nature's great King, through endless years the same ;
>   We are Thy children, we alone, of all
>   On earth's broad ways, that wander to and fro,
>   Bearing Thine image whereso'er we go.
>   Vehicle of the universal Word, that flows
>   Through all, and in the light celestial glows
>   Of stars both great and small ;  O King of kings,
>   Chaos to Thee is order :  in Thine eyes
>   The unloved is lovely, Who didst harmonize
>   Things evil with things good, that there should be
>   One Word through all things everlastingly." [1]

Thus Stoicism gave to its adherents the conception that man could come into a close relation with God ; one Divine Word was the essence of both, and by fostering the divine within themselves men could come into contact with the Divine Mind. A later Stoic, Seneca the Roman, born about the beginning of the Christian era, writes thus : " A divine force has come

---

[1] Tr. J. Adam.

down to earth, a heavenly power, by which the soul, with its splendid powers of thought, raises itself above all lower things. As the rays of the sun touch the earth indeed, but have their true home in that place whence they came forth, so it is with the great and holy Spirit which is sent down hither in order that we may learn to known the Deity better. God is near you, with you, within you . . . a holy Spirit dwells within us, spectator of our evil and our good, and guardian." [1]  Again he says : " God comes to men, nay ! nearer still ! He comes into men. No mind is good without God. Divine seeds are sown in human bodies : if they are well tended they will grow up into the likeness of That from which they sprang." [2]

Epictetus, the freed slave and Stoic teacher, tells his hearers that all things are a unity : things earthly are in sympathy with things heavenly, the souls of men are bound up and in touch with God and are parts of Him.

To the Stoics, as to other mystics, purity of heart and life was an indispensable condition of spiritual attainment ; in their view, the inner spirit must free itself from everything individual, from emotion as from sensation, in order to become one with the Divine Reason. Only by the surrender of all that could be counted as its own could the spirit of man make its way to, and become one with, the Universal Spirit.

Plutarch, who lived in the first century of our era, reckoned himself a disciple of Plato, but he modified the views of his great teacher and combined them with those of other great spiritual thinkers among the Greeks. The One Ultimate Reason which controls the universe is by him called the One and the Absolute, the great energising Force, the World-Soul. The soul

[1] *Ep.* 41.　　　　　　　[2] *Ep.* 73.

of man is immortal, since we have within us something of the Divine, some likeness to God. He teaches that there is some undefined Spirit interpenetrating the visible world, which speaks to the individual soul, but is comprehended only by those who have attuned their body to be able to hear. Here again we have the mystic ideal of purification in order to become godlike. Not everyone understands the nature of the Divine and many confuse God with His manifestations. Men must be pointed higher, says Plutarch, and he bids them go upward and see the truth of their dream, the real Being.

But the school of classical philosophy, which had the most far-reaching influence on Mysticism, was undoubtedly that of the Neo-Platonists, and among them the master-mind was Plotinus, who was born in Egypt at the beginning of the third century of the Christian era. He gathers up the threads of the old Greek philosophy, the ideas of Plato and Aristotle and the Stoics, and in his teaching we find a mystical doctrine of great power and spiritual insight, the work of the profoundest thinker not only of his own age but for many ages to come. At the heart of his doctrine is his belief in the essential unity of the universe, " God is not external to anyone." There is in the universe a movement down from God manwards and a movement up from man Godwards.

The first Principle in the Godhead is Primeval Being, the source and ground of all being, transcending all known attributes and even the idea of existence, the One, the Highest Good, Perfect Beauty. From this Primeval Principle, the first emanation is Universal Mind, the world of Ideas, containing the archetypes of all things in the phenomenal world, the Over-mind of whom all minds partake. From Mind comes the second emanation, Soul, the Universal Soul, which manifests itself in individual souls, and gives existence to the phenomenal world, and these therefore share in the Divine life. So the Godhead, to Plotinus, is a Trinity, in which the first Person is the Absolute, the second Mind, and the third Soul.

By the same way by which it descended, the individual soul can ascend again to its home in God. It must first come to itself by the process of purification, the practice of virtue which aims at likeness to God and leads up to Him. Only the pure in heart can hope to see God, says Plotinus : " If the eye that adventures the vision be dimmed by vice, impure or weak and unable in its cowardly blenching to see the uttermost brightness, then it sees nothing, even though another point to what lies plain before it. To any vision must be brought an eye adapted to what is to be seen, and having some likeness to it. Never did eye see the sun unless it had first become sun-like and never can the soul have vision of the First Beauty unless itself be beautiful.

" Therefore let each become godlike and each beautiful who cares to see God and Beauty." [1]

To attain this end, the soul must hold itself above all passions and affections, it must separate itself from the body, from the system of sense with desires and impulses, all that sets definitely towards the mortal, and so the soul will accomplish the first stage of return and be restored to the unity of Universal Soul.

The soul has now passed by the Purgative Way and is cleansed from the senses and from desire, but it

[1] *Ennead*, i. 9, tr. S. Mackenna.

must ascend farther to that which is nearer to the One than Universal Soul, to Mind, after whom and from whom Soul is. Here the spirit can rest awhile in the realm of pure thought, engaged in contemplation. Here it can find a true unity with the All. " The Soul thus cleansed," says Plotinus, " is all Idea and Reason, wholly free of body, intellective, entirely of that divine order from which the wellspring of Beauty rises and all the race of Beauty. Hence the Soul heightened to the Intellectual Principle is beautiful to all its power. And it is just to say that in the Soul's becoming a good and beautiful thing is its becoming like to God, for from the Divine comes all the Beauty and all the Good in beings." [1] This is the illuminative life, in which the soul sees clearly : " All things are transparent, and there is nothing dark or resisting, but every one is manifest to everyone internally."

But the ascent is not yet accomplished ; the soul must still press on to the final Good, the vision of God in His perfect Beauty. " To attain it," says Plotinus again, " is for those that will take the upward path, who will divest themselves of all that we have put on in our descent—until passing, on the upward way, all that is other than God, each in the solitude of himself shall behold that solitary-dwelling Existence, the Apart, the Unmingled, the Pure, that from Which all things depend, for which all look and live and act and know, the Source of Life and of Intellection and of Being.

And one that shall know this vision—with what passion of love shall he not be seized, with what pang of desire, what longing to be molten into one with This, what wondering delight ! If he that has

[1] *Ennead,* v. 8, 4.

never seen this Being must hunger for It as for all
his welfare, he that has known must love and reverence
It as the very Beauty ; he will be flooded with awe
and gladness—he loves with a veritable love, with
sharp desire : all other loves than this he must despise,
and disdain all that once seemed fair.

And for This, the sternest and the uttermost combat
is set before the Souls ; all our labour is for This,
lest we be left without part in this noblest vision,
which to attain is to be blessed in the blissful sight,
which to fail of is to fail utterly." [1]

The soul has reached the end of its quest and has
attained to the Unitive life ; it has become one with its
Divine origin. " The Soul restored to Likeness
goes to its Like and holds of the Supreme all that
Soul can hold. This is not to say that in this plunging
into the Divine the Soul reaches nothingness—by
this way, this that leads to the Good, it finds itself ;
when it is the Divine, it is truly itself, no longer a thing
among things. It abandons Being to become a
Beyond-Being when its converse is in the Supreme.
He who knows himself to have become such, knows
himself now an image of the Supreme ; and when the
phantasm has returned to the Original, the journey is
achieved. Suppose him to fall again from the Vision,
he will call up the virtue within him and, seeing
himself all glorious again, he will take his upward
flight once more, through virtue to the Divine Mind,
through the Wisdom There to the Supreme. And
this is the life of the Gods and of Godlike men, a life
without love of the world, a flight of the Alone to the
Alone." [2]

<hr />

[1] *Ennead*, i. 7, tr. Mackenna.
[2] *Ibid.,* vi. 9, 11.

It was little wonder that succeeding mystics took Plotinus as their guide and leader on the Mystic Way, and how much they owed to his deep insight and his clear exposition of that which he had seen and known we shall realise in the chapters that follow.

# CHAPTER V

# MYSTICISM IN THE EARLY CHRISTIAN CHURCH

THE Mysticism of the early Christian Fathers, though it was based mainly upon the Old and New Testaments, contains many Greek elements, and in their efforts to formulate a theology for the young Christian Church we see plainly how much they owed to Hellenistic culture and environment and, most of all, to Platonism and its later developments.

The first of whom we may take note in this connection is Irenæus (A.D. 130–202), bishop of Lyons, who set forth his conception of the relation between man and God in a treatise called *Against Heresies*. He conceives of God the Father as Perfection, and of the Son as the Logos, carrying out the Father's behests. There is a true kinship between God and His World, and the image of God has never really been lost ; it is part of the nature of man, and man can therefore attain to likeness to God. Through the Incarnation, this human, perishable nature has become deified and death has been changed into immortal life. So, by the redemptive work of the Son, man can attain to union with God : " The Lord pours out the Spirit of the Father for the union and communion of God and man, imparting God to man through the Spirit and raising man on the other hand to God." To participate in God is to see Him and enjoy His goodness. A man who truly lives is the glory of God, and to live truly is to behold the vision of God.

Clement of Alexandria, born about A.D. 150, aimed at formulating a philosophy of religion : he speaks of a " Gnosis " whereby the Christian who was fitted to receive it might be initiated into the higher mysteries of his faith.  The true Gnostic, by means of this mystic knowledge, could rise above earthly passions and desires to the goal of the Christian achievement, the contemplation of God.  " It is," he says, " the greatest of all lessons to know oneself.  For if one knows himself he will know God, and knowing God, he will be made like unto God."  This knowledge is not merely intellectual, it is won by mortification and contempt of the world, and by a self-conquest which leads to purity, and is inspired by love : " For the more a man loves the more deeply does he pene- trate into God " ; and again : " What more need of courage and desire to him, who has attained the affinity to the impassible God, which arises from love, and by love has enrolled himself among the Friends of God ? "

Like other mystic teachers, Clement points out the three stages of the Way.  The would-be Gnostic must by discipline rid himself of passion ; he who would hold converse with God must have his soul immaculate and stainlessly pure, it being essential to have made himself perfectly good.  Having passed by the way of Purgation to enlightenment, the Gnostic proceeds thence to the Unitive life, that is, the life lived habitually and without effort in harmony with the Will of God, a life of abiding peace and joy. " Wherefore," says Clement in his *Stromateis*, " the Gnosis doth easily translate the soul to the divine and holy which is akin to it, and by its own light conveys a man through the mystic stages, until it restores him at last to the supernal place of rest, teaching him who is pure in heart to gaze upon God, face to face, with perfect science and understanding.  For in this consisteth the perfection of the gnostic soul that, rising above all purification and service, it should be with God." [1]

Clement, in his writings, constantly uses the language of the mystics : he holds that the gift of immortality means sharing in the Godhead, and he is responsible for the introduction of this doctrine of deification into Christian mysticism. He also writes of mental prayer, saying first that prayer is converse with God, and then that prayer may be uttered without the voice, by concentrating the whole spiritual nature within, on expression by the mind, in undisturbed turning towards God.

There is much of a mystical nature in the writings of Origen (A.D. 185–254). To him God is beyond Being, He is Transcendent, pure Spirit, eternal, unchangeable, immaterial. The world had eternally emanated from God and therefore exists in God as its cause. The second Person in the Godhead Origen calls the " Idea of Ideas," the one through Whom God works spiritually, Who is the basis of the many, and here we see plainly the influence of Greek philosophy. He takes a sacramental view of Nature, as Plato did : all that is the work of God bears His impress, and thereby the soul—which at first was perfect, but has fallen from its high estate—is taught and raised to the contemplation of the invisible and the eternal. The world, that is to say, is the means of ascent whereby the mind of man can rise to understand spiritual mysteries. Therefore, though God as Transcendent is in one sense incomprehensible, in another sense He is comprehensible, and it is possible to draw nearer and nearer to Him until at

[1] *Stromateis,* vii. x. 57.

last we shall be able to behold Him as He is. Every spirit must return at the last to God, for that which is spiritual is immortal. The Good, that is, God, alone exists, evil has no real existence, so when the soul has passed beyond the things of earth and beyond the heavens, it will have a vision of the Ideal world as it is in God, when the soul shall have passed beyond the mere symbols to see the nature of the Ideal and look upon the beauty of Truth itself.

So, at the final consummation, Origen says that the saints will understand all the mysteries of the Divine ordinances, Love will save them from the possibility of defection, and at last God will be all in all.

But the greatest of all these early mystics of the Church was St. Augustine, who joined to a great intellectual capacity for penetrating the mysteries of things divine, a love of God that was a consuming passion. He acknowledged but one desire, which was to know God and the soul and nothing more. He gives us the record of the transformation of his own soul by the grace of God, and into the fabric of the Christian faith he weaves the strands he has gathered up from his early researches into Greek philosophy and religion. God is to him above all that can be said or expressed, and is therefore best adored in silence. He is the only Substance, the Cause of all being, and St. Augustine, following Plotinus, speaks of the Beauty of God, and of the Divine Nature as the source of all that is Good, and True, and Beautiful: " All that is beautiful comes from the highest Beauty, which is God." As the soul had come from God, to God it must return, and the stages of the ascent were by way of purgation and illumination until the goal of union was reached.

He taught that there could be direct intercourse between the soul and God, by means of that spiritual sense, the " eye " of the soul, the " ear " of the mind : " God speaks with a man, not by means of some audible creature dinning in his ears—not by these does God speak, but by the truth itself, if anyone is prepared to hear with the mind rather than with the body. He speaks to that part of man which is better than all else in him, and than which God Himself alone is better " [1] ; and in the same treatise, *The City of God*, he says that the incorporeal soul is illumined by the incorporeal light of the Wisdom of God, as the body of the air is illumined by corporeal light.

The soul seeks to return to God, to the life of the blessed, because it has some dim memory—here we have the Platonic idea of recollection—of the time when it dwelt with God. " We could not love it, that blessed life," he says, " unless we knew it." Like all the other mystics, St. Augustine assumes that the soul must make its ascent by gradual stages, of which he mentions seven, but the higher are the familiar ones of purgation and illumination leading to union, for the vision and contemplation of truth means a return to God. To prepare to see the Truth he bids the soul destroy in itself all that is contrary to truth ; to see that Light the inward eye must be prepared, to drink of that Fountain the inward thirst must be kindled.

Then when the soul has been purified and the eye can see clearly, the mystic can hope to attain that for which he has sought. " If to anyone should grow hushed the tumult of the flesh, hushed the images of earth, and if the very soul should be hushed to

[1] *The City of God*, xi. 2.

itself and were by cessation of thought of self to pass beyond itself—if we should hear Him, and in the flight of thought we touched upon the eternal Wisdom that abideth over all things : if this were continued and other visions of a nature by far inferior were taken away, and this one alone should ravish and absorb and enwrap the beholder of it amid inward joys, so that life everlasting might be of such a kind, as was that moment of comprehension for which we sighed : were not this an ' enter thou into the joy of thy Lord ' ? " [1]   It was to this end that Augustine prepared himself, and this was the vision that he dreamed of and to which at last he attained : " With the flash of one trembling glance my mind arrived at That which Is.   And then I saw Thy invisible things understood by the things which are made."   When the soul has seen Ultimate Reality it realises the vanity of all things under the sun.   " If the glorious cup of the Lord intoxicate you," says Augustine, who has drunk of that cup, " it shall be seen indeed in a certain alienation of your mind, but an alienation from the things of earth to those of heaven." [2]

A writer who had a far-reaching influence on all later Christian mysticism was Dionysius, the " Areopagite " so-called, though it is clear from internal evidence that his writings originated about the end of the fifth century A.D.   His mysticism is plainly derived from Hellenistic sources in the main, though he makes use also of Jewish ideas, and the whole is adapted to form a highly developed system of Christian mysticism.   God the Father he identifies with the Neo-Platonic Monad : He is sublimely Transcendent, the ultimate Divine Source in Whom

---

[1] *Confessions*, ix. 10.          [2] *Enar. in Ps.*, ciii. 3, 13.

all Beauty and Goodness meet, the cause of all things that are, from Whom life is given to all lower orders of existence. Therefore, whatever is, is part of the Divine Life and Love, which for ever purifies, enlightens and makes perfect and so draws all back again to Itself, the Source. To Dionysius the Divine Love is " an eternal circle, from goodness, through goodness and to goodness."

In his book called *The Celestial Hierarchy*, he gives an account of the ninefold order of the heavenly hierarchy, which consists of the Seraphim, Cherubim and Thrones ; the Dominations, Virtues, Powers ; the Principalities, Archangels, Angels. God is their Head, and their office is to raise mankind to God through purification, illumination and perfection. Dionysius wrote also *The Ecclesiastical Hierarchy*, of which Christ is the Head. This is also ninefold, consisting of Baptism, Communion, Holy Chrism ; the Bishops, Presbyters, Deacons ; monks, laity, catechumens. The highest in each of these triads represents Perfection, the second Illumination, and the third Purification. God, though He be unknown, can yet be reached, and the aim of the soul, purified, illumined and perfected, is union with Him, and this is achieved by a gnosis, a mystic intuition which is above the intellect. " By laying aside all mental energies," says Dionysius in his treatise *Concerning the Divine Names*, " and by all-pure contemplation the soul shares in that super-essential Light, in which all knowledge pre-exists, and enters into a union above thought, above states of consciousness, above knowledge." [1]

When the mystic has left behind all things in the

[1] i. 4.

worlds of sense and of intellect, he can enter into that Divine Darkness, which is in truth Light unapproachable, dark through excess of light. In his book *Concerning Mystic Theology*, Dionysius bids the mystic in the intent practice of mystic contemplation to " leave behind the senses and the operations of the intellect and all things that the senses or the intellect can perceive and all things which are not and things which are and strain upwards in unknowing, as far as may be, towards the union with Him Who is above all being and knowledge. For by unceasing and absolute withdrawal from thyself and all things in purity, abandoning all and set free from all, thou wilt be borne up to the ray of the divine Darkness that surpasseth all being. Unto this Darkness which is beyond Light we pray that we may come, and through loss of sight and knowledge may see and know That Which transcends sight and knowledge by the very fact of not seeing and knowing : for this is real sight and knowledge." [1]

To the mystic to whom God has manifested the vision of Himself unveiled, there is granted union, the goal of the mystic quest. " They who are free and untrammelled enter into the true Mystical Darkness of Unknowing, whence all perception of understanding is excluded, and abide in That which is intangible and invisible, being wholly absorbed in Him Who is beyond all, and are united in their higher part to Him Who is wholly unknowable and Whom, by understanding nothing, they understand after a manner above all intelligence." [2]

It was this Dionysian system of mysticism, introduced into Europe in the ninth century, which formed

[1] *Mystical Theology*, i. ii.     [2] *Ibid.*, i.

the pattern for the later mysticism of the Christian Church, and its influence was widespread. The goal of this later mysticism was the Beatific Vision, absorption into—union with—the Godhead, while its basis was that from which Dionysius started, the belief that the soul itself was divine, coming from God, and that when it should come to itself, through purification and illumination to perfection, it could also return to God, its Source.

# CHAPTER VI

# MYSTICISM IN THE ORIENT

AT an early period there arose in China a form of religion which contained the chief elements of a fully developed mystical doctrine : the " Teaching " known as Tao-ism. Our knowledge of it is derived from the mystic treatise called the *Tao-Teh-King*, the *Treatise of the Way and of Virtue*, the authorship of which has traditionally been attributed to Lao-tse (Laocius), who was born in 604 B.C.

He held an official post in the state of Chou, but gave it up and retired from the world and from the company of his fellow men, in order to be free to commune with his own heart and to meditate upon the nature of reality. He says of himself and his doctrines : " It is very easy to comprehend my teachings and to put them into practice, yet the world can neither understand nor practise them. Those who understand me are few, and on that account I am the more distinguished. Hence the Holy Man wears coarse garments, but carries a jewel in his bosom." [1]

The goal of humanity is union with Reality, and the Holy Men, who are perfected, are those who attain to this goal.

" Tao," which is literally the Way, is used by Lao-tse to mean the Ultimate Reality, the principle and law of Nature, the First Cause of all existence. It is nameless and inexpressible, yet all-pervading. Tao represents the Godhead unmanifested, but from it emanates the Mother of all things, from whom the world has taken its beginning. All things under

[1] *Tao-Teh-King*, lxx.

Heaven derive their being from Tao in the form of existence, and Tao in the form of Existence sprang from Tao in the form of non-existence. " Tao produced Unity ; Unity produced Duality ; Duality produced Trinity and Trinity produced all things." [1]

Tao is not only the Ultimate Cause, but also the Sustainer of all that exists. " Tao gives life to all creatures, nourishes them, develops them and fosters them ; perfects them, matures them, tends them and protects them." [2] Tao, as Non-Existence, is eternally inactive, yet, through its manifestation, as Existence, it leaves nothing undone. So too the one who would attain to it should neither strive nor be neglectful of his duty to the community.

Tao is not only the Source whence all things proceed, it is also the goal to which all things tend to return, and there is hope for all men, for the possession of it and reunion with it is potentially available for all who truly desire redemption thereby. Tao is a sanctuary where all can find refuge, " the good man's priceless treasure and the protector of him who is not good. It may be daily sought and found, and by its help the guilty can be saved from their sins." [3]

It is clear, then, that Tao is transcendent considered as the Ultimate Nameless Reality, but immanent considered as manifested by emanation in the universe. But in all this there is no idea of a personal God, with a bond of relationship between Himself and man.

The Way to be trodden by those who seek to become possessed of Tao is set forth clearly, and the writer observes that it is very plain, but people prefer the bypaths. The Way, as always, means Purgation.

---

[1] *Tao-Teh-King*, xlii.     [2] *Ibid.*, li.     [3] *Ibid.*, lxii.

"Only the one who is eternally free from earthly desires can apprehend the spiritual essence of Tao ; he who is ever hindered by passions can see no more than its outward manifestation." [1]   Again he writes : "He who sustains and disciplines his soul by subordinating the animal instincts to reason will be able to escape dissolution. By purification, by cleansing and by deep intuition he can be freed from his faults." [2]   The holy man takes heed therefore to what is inward not what is outward ; he turns aside from the objective and holds to the subjective. By self-conquest he will attain to Illumination. "To see oneself is to be enlightened. Mighty is the one who conquers himself." [3]   Lao-tse urges all who follow the Mystic Way to use the light which is within them to gain enlightenment. Knowledge of the law that all must return to their Source, that is, knowledge of the true unity of all existence, is Illumination.

By carrying out these precepts the seeker reaches that state of "purity and stillness" which is the correct principle for mankind. "The man who is in harmony with the principle of Tao is untouched alike by favour and disgrace, by benefits and injuries, by honour and contempt." The perfected man can now live the unitive life, partaking of the properties of Tao, becoming free from the laws imposed upon the uninitiated, able to act as the instrument through which Tao works. "Without going out of doors one may know the whole world ; without looking out of the window one may see the Way of Heaven— so without travelling the holy man shall comprehend ; without labour he shall achieve." [4]   The holy man,

[1] *Tao-Teh-King*, i.      [2] *Ibid.*, x.
[3] *Ibid.*, xxxiii.      [4] *Ibid.*, xlvii.

that is, the mystic, embraces Unity, and so becomes a model for all under Heaven, free from self-assertion and self-glorification, yet shining forth by the sanctity of his life as greater than all others.

Having attained to union, he abides therein. " One possessed of Tao endures for ever." He has consciously returned to the Absolute, become one with the All, attained to the Mystery of the Unity.

Other teachers of Taoism followed Lao-tse, among them Lieh-tse, who flourished in the fifth century B.C., and who taught that Taoism meant a selfless identification with the life of nature, a doctrine which resulted in Quietism. He also developed the idea, so common in the history of Mysticism, that miracles could be wrought by the perfectly pure, an idea which led to the weaving of fantastic legends about the persons and lives of the Taoist saints.

Another great Taoist teacher was Chwang-tse or Sancius (c. 330 B.C.), who taught that Tao was the divine First Principle, but that T'ien, God or Heaven, was the great First Cause. The truth of life, he taught, is to be found when self-consciousness and self-determination are completely lost.

Taoism, in its primitive form, has many elements in common with Brahman philosophy, and in its view of the ultimate unity it resembles the doctrine of Plotinus. But it degenerated later, even before the Christian era, into a system of charlatanry, concerned with magic, and including the traffic in charms and exorcisms with which it is still concerned. In imitation of Buddhist institutions it established temples and monasteries for its votaries in the fifth century A.D. and in many ways assimilated itself to Buddhism.

Space will not allow of more than a brief reference to the mystical elements to be found in the faiths of India, though Indian mysticism is perhaps the oldest of all. The characteristics of this mysticism, as it is found in Hinduism, are the desire for escape from selfhood and the evils of the world, and the belief in " karma," the doctrine of works, which maintains that an individual at any given time is the result of all that he has done before, whether good or evil, and with this is linked up the doctrine of metem-psychosis, the belief in successive rebirths. So that the Hindu quest is to escape from the possibility of rebirth and attain to union with Infinity, the Ultimate.

In the earliest Vedic period there are few indications of the mystical attitude of mind, but the Bhagavad-Gītā, the " Divine Lay," which belongs to about the third century B.C., and which brings together the doctrines of the Upanishads, the Sānkhya and the Yoga, contains a clearly stated mystical doctrine. At the summit of all existence is the Supreme Being, the Holy One, the Eternal Creative Word. The universe has reality because it shares the spiritual nature of the Absolute Spirit, Brahma ; all souls come forth from Him, and will return to Him and abide with Him in union. By knowledge and self-discipline, but chiefly by the spirit of loving devotion, will the soul be enabled to return to its home in God. " The man who casts off all desires and walks without desire, with no thought of a Mine and of an I, comes into peace," and again the Lord speaks, saying, " He who does My work, who is given over to Me, who is devoted to Me, void of attachment, without hatred to any born being, comes unto Me."

A late exponent of this school of thought was Kabīr,

born about 1440, who was undoubtedly affected by
Islam and Islamic mysticism : he held that salvation
was to be attained, not by knowledge or good works,
but only by loving faith.  He maintains that God
has drawn near to men and can be reached without
the mediation of orthodox religion, whether Hindu
or Moslem.  He says, in one of his poems :

" The whole world does its works and commits its errors ;
   but few are the lovers who know the Belovèd.
The devout seeker is he who mingles in his heart the
   double currents of love and detachment : like the
   mingling of the streams of Ganges and Jumna.
In his heart the sacred water flows day and night : and
   thus the round of births and deaths is brought to an end.
Behold what wonderful rest is in the Supreme Spirit !
   and he enjoys it who makes himself meet for it." [1]

And elsewhere he writes :

" If you merge your life in the Ocean of Life, you will find
   life in the Supreme Land of Bliss."

He gives a beautiful description of the love of the
mystic for the Beloved in some of his verses :

" How could the love between Thee and me sever ?
As the leaf of the lotus abides on the water : so Thou
   art my Lord and I am Thy servant,
As the night-bird Chakar gazes all night at the moon :
   so Thou art my Lord and I am Thy servant." [2]

And once more on this theme :

" Subtle is the path of love !
Therein is no asking and no not-asking,
There one loses one's self at His feet,
There one is immersed in the joy of the seeking :
   plunged in the deeps of love as the fish in the water." [3]

[1] *Kabīr's Poems*, tr. Tagore, xvii.
[2] *Ibid.*, xxxiv.                     [3] *Ibid.*, lv.

Kabīr is a thoroughgoing pantheist, seeing God in all things : " The Lord is in me, the Lord is in you— seek for Him within you " ; and God, to him, is Love: " One Love it is that pervades the whole world, few there are who know it fully." He is Beauty, too : " How shall I find words for the beauty of my Beloved ? For He is merged in all beauty " ; and at the last, to the sound of the music of the meeting of soul with soul, the music of the forgetting of sorrows, the music that transcends all coming in and all going forth, the vision of the Beloved, in all His beauty, will be revealed to the true lover, within his own heart.

Buddhism, which had its rise in the seventh century B.C. and has spread through India and the Far East, also points to a mystic way of salvation. The foundation of its doctrine is fourfold :

(1) There is Suffering everywhere in the world ; (2) the Cause of Suffering is desire or craving ; (3) the Remedy for Suffering is the complete Extinction of craving ; (4) the Path that leads to this extinction is the Eightfold Noble Path, which is in truth a ladder for the mystic, leading upward to the goal, Nirvāna. Existence is conceived of as a burning and Nirvāna is the dying down of the flames.

" All things," says the Buddha, " are on fire, and with what ? With the fire of passion, the fire of hatred, the fire of infatuation ; with birth, old age, death, sorrows, lamentation, misery, grief and despair are they on fire.

" Wherein does Nirvāna consist ? When the fire of lust is extinct, that is Nirvāna ; when the fires of hatred and infatuation are extinct, that is Nirvāna ;

when pride, false belief and all other passions are extinct, that is Nirvāna." [1]

The guide along the Eightfold Path is Love: "All the means available as grounds for right conduct are not worth a sixteenth part of the liberation of the heart through love. That outshines them all in radiance and absorbs them into itself as the radiance of the moon outshines that of all the stars." [2]   Yet Buddhism has no God ; the knowledge that leads to enlightenment and so to Nirvāna is not the direct intuition of the Absolute, it is a clear understanding of the true character of the Supremely Righteous Law and conformity thereto.

Nirvāna can be attained in this life, and for that one who has attained here and now, in the next life there will be cessation of Becoming, and when Becoming has ceased, Birth will cease and with its cessation old age, death, grief, lamentation, pain, sorrow and despair cease to exist. Yet there is some claim to reality for Nirvāna, and Sir Edwin Arnold, in *The Light of Asia*, expresses it thus :

> " Such is the law which moves to righteousness,
>     Which none at last can turn aside or stay ;
>     The heart of it is Love, the end of it
>     Is Peace and Consummation sweet.   *Obey.*"

And again :
                              " He goes

>     Unto Nirvāna, He is one with Life,
>     Yet lives not.   He is blest, ceasing to be.
>     Om, mani padme, om !  the Dewdrop slips
>     Into the shining sea !
>                         Seeking nothing, he gains all,
>     Foregoing self, the Universe grows " I,"
>     If any teach Nirvāna is to cease,
>     Say unto such they lie.

[1] *Jātalas*, Intro., i. 58, tr. Warner.   [2] *Itivuttaka*, p. 19.

If any teach Nirvāna is to live,
Say unto such they err ; not knowing this,
Nor what light shines beyond their broken lamps,
Nor lifeless, timeless bliss.''

\*       \*       \*

Ṣūfīsm, or Islamic mysticism, developed at an early stage in the history of Islam, and was due, in its earliest form at least, to the widespread ascetic tendencies of the first century of the Islamic era, tendencies which in a large measure were derived from the example of Christian asceticism. It was due also to the revolt of the more spiritually minded Moslems against the formalism and the unsatisfying theology of their creed. It was adopted at first by individuals, and then by small groups, and gradually became an organised system. It represented at first, and indeed has always represented, a Way of life, but it further developed into a mystic-philosophic system of idealised pantheism. The Ṣūfī held that it was man's business to eliminate the element of Not-Being and to attain to that union with God, that absorption into the Divine which was possible, in some measure at least, even in this life. This could be attained only by the conquest of self, and self could be conquered only through the power of Love. Only by Love could Not-Being be done away, only by means of Love could man's soul return to its divine source and find the end of its quest in reunion with the One, the Truth.

The preparation for those who sought to follow the Mystic Way was the life of Purgation, a life of asceticism, through which the carnal soul might be purified from its sins, which had their source in the desires of self. When cleansed from these sensual desires, the soul could enter on the Path which was destined to lead it to union with the Divine. The Way to the Ṣūfī, as to other mystics, was made up of a number of stages, in its passage through which the soul acquired certain qualities which enabled it to rise higher and higher, until at last, partly through its own efforts and partly through the grace of God, it reached the heavenly gnosis, and the mystic, thus enlightened, was enabled to contemplate the Vision of God Himself and to abide in Him for ever.

The great Moslem theologian, al-Ghazālī (A.D. 1058–1111), seeking to prove that the mystical element in Islam is its most essential and vital part, asserts that the Ṣūfī, that is, the mystic, must cut off his attachments to the world completely and free his heart from them, until their existence or non-existence is alike to him. Then he should go into retreat alone and occupy his mind with nothing but God, using at first symbols and then discarding these, so that he is prepared for all that God may reveal to him. Then the Light of God will shine upon him, and that vision will be like a blinding flash of lightning, indescribable, ineffable.

To the Ṣūfīs, as to all Moslems, the Unity of God was the central doctrine of their faith, but the Ṣūfīs attached a mystical meaning of their own to this, which for them became the doctrine of Unification, the abnegation of the personal will in the eternal Will of God. The Persian mystic Abū Saʿīd b. Abī al-Khayr (d. 1049) laid it down that " thou canst not believe in God until thou dost deny thyself that self which keeps thee far from God Most High, and which says, ' So and So has done thee an injury and such a one has treated thee well.' All this leads to dependence on creatures and all this is polytheism. The creatures are nothing, the Friend is everything —when thou hast said ' One ' thou must not again say ' Two.' The right faith is to say God and therein to stand fast. Whatever thou dost see or say, see and say from what is existent, which never ceases to be. Love that One Who, when thou shalt cease to be, will not Himself cease to be, that thou too mayst become one who will never cease to be." [1]

The Ṣūfī had much to say of Love, that disinterested passion which consumed the mystic with longing for the consummation of love in union with the Beloved. " Love," said one of them, " means to give all that thou hast to Him Whom thou lovest, so that nothing remains to thee of thine own "; and another : " Love is a fire in the heart consuming all save the Beloved." Of the effects of this Love upon the mystic, a Ṣūfī wrote to Abū Yazīd Bisṭāmī, a well-known mystic : " What do you say of one who drinks a single drop of the ocean of Love and becomes intoxicated ? " and the other wrote in reply : " What do you say of one who, if all the oceans in the world were filled with the wine of Love, would drink them all and still cry for more to slake his thirst ? " [2]

Love leads the mystic to knowledge of the Divine mysteries ; those who love and abide in God, to whom He is nearer than to any others, to them is given the vision of God unveiled, and they see Him with the eye of certainty. From the vision the mystic passes into Union, and of this al-Junayd of Baghdad says :

[1] Munawwar, *Asrār al-Tawḥīd*, p. 371.
[2] *Kashf al-Maḥjūb*, ed. R. A. Nicholson, p. 187.

" God gives to the gnostic (i.e. the mystic) the sharp desire to behold His Essence, then knowledge becomes vision and vision revelation, and revelation contemplation and contemplation existence (with and in God). Words are hushed to silence, life becomes death, signs are effaced. Mortality is ended and immortality is made perfect. Weariness and care cease, the elements perish, and there remains what will not cease, as time that is timeless ceases not." [1]

Of all the early Ṣūfīs, the most typical mystic was Rābi'a of Basra (A.D. 717–801), described by her Persian biographer as " that one on fire with love and longing, that one enamoured of the desire to approach her Lord and be consumed in His glory, that woman who lost herself in union with the Divine," who prayed, " O my Lord, if I worship Thee from fear of Hell, burn me in Hell ; and if I worship Thee from Hope of Paradise, exclude me thence ; but if I worship Thee for thine own sake, then withhold not from me Thine Eternal Beauty," and that Vision was not denied to her, for in verses of hers which have come down to us, she tells how God has shewn Himself to her unveiled, because of her great love to Him.[2]

Al-Hallāj, a courageous and original thinker among the Ṣūfīs, asserted : " I am He whom I love, and He whom I love is I " ; and said further : " If ye do not recognise God, at least recognise His signs. I am that sign, I am the Creative Truth," and for his boldness he suffered martyrdom at Baghdad in A.D. 922. He was the precursor of those later Ṣūfīs who

[1] *Asrār al-Tawḥīd*, p. 378.
[2] M. Smith, *Rābi'a the Mystic and her Fellow Saints in Islām*.

developed a theosophic doctrine which was pure pantheism. To them, God, the Absolute, Unmingled Good, Supreme Beauty, the true Beloved, is the only Reality ; He is Pure Being, and nothing beside Him has any existence except as His reflection : the Universe is but a mirror reflecting the Absolute Beauty and man himself the most polished mirror capable of giving back the most faithful reflection. But the mirror itself is also one with the only Reality. In one of the quatrains of Abū Saʻīd, God declares :

> " I am Love and I am the Beloved : and no less am I the Lover,
> I am the Mirror and I am Beauty : therefore behold Me in Myself."

So also Shabistarī, in the *Rose-Garden of Mystery*, says : " In God there is no duality. In that Presence ' I ' and ' we ' and ' thou ' do not exist, ' I ' and ' we ' and ' thou ' and ' he ' become one. The Quest and the Way and the Seeker become one," and some of the most beautiful verses in the mystical poetry of the Arabs and Persians deal with this theme. For example, Ibn al-Fārid, the greatest of Arab mystical poets, in one of his odes, speaking of the Beloved, says :

> " Though He be gone, mine every limb beholds Him
> In every charm and grace and loveliness :
> In music of the lute and flowing reed
> Mingled in consort with melodious airs ;
> And in green hollows where in cool of eve
> Gazelles roam browsing, or at break of morn ;
> And where the gathered clouds let fall their rain
> Upon a flowing carpet woven of blooms ;

And where at dawn with softly trailing skirts
The zephyr brings to me His balm most sweet ;
And when in kisses from the flagon's mouth
I suck wine-dew beneath a pleasant shade." [1]

An even more complete pantheism is set forth in
the beautiful lines of Jāmī, the Persian mystic (A.D.
1414–1492) :

" Each speck of matter did He constitute
A mirror, causing each one to reflect
The beauty of His visage.  From the rose
Flashed forth His beauty, and the nightingale,
Beholding it, loved madly.  From that fire
The candle drew the lustre which beguiles
The moth to immolation.  On the sun
His beauty shone, and straightway from the wave
The lotus reared its head.  Each shining lock
Of Layla's hair attracted Majnūn's heart
Because some ray Divine reflected shone
In her fair face.—'Twas He to Shīrīn's lips
Who lent that sweetness, which had power to steal
The heart from Parvīz and from Farhād life.
His Beauty everywhere doth shew itself,
And through the forms of earthly beauties shines
Obscured as through a veil——
                              Where'er thou seest a veil,
Beneath that veil He hides." [2]

Hence these pantheistic Ṣūfīs declare that the Unreal
is the bridge to the Real, and hold, like Plato, that
by means of forms man can ascend to the Essence.
By self-stripping the mystic learns Love, at first of
earthly beauty, then, when he perceives that this is
but the reflection of the Eternal Beauty, his love is

[1] Diwān, tr. R. A. Nicholson.
[2] Tr. E. G. Browne.

set upon that One, and ceases not to aspire in burning longing until it is consummated in abiding Union, when—

> " Lover, Beloved and Love are one at last,
>   And He, the One, the Real is All in All."

# CHAPTER VII

# SOME MYSTICS OF THE EARLY MIDDLE AGES

THE Middle Ages in Europe saw a great development of Mysticism, and we can choose only a few among the mystics of this period to serve as representatives of those who taught a mystical doctrine and followed the Mystic Way.

The first to be considered is St. Bernard of Clairvaux (A.D. 1090–1153), a great contemplative who teaches how man can attain to the knowledge and vision of God. It is possible, he maintains, for man, by abstraction from earthly things, by self-emptying, and by a love which desires not merely vision but penetration of the heart by God, to rise to contemplation of the Divine, when the soul will be permitted a clear vision of the Divine Majesty for a brief moment, with the swiftness of a lightning flash. In this mystic union the soul is set aglow with the love of God and has a momentary foretaste of heaven. St. Bernard speaks of God's revelation of Himself in the beauties of nature, and adds : " God has another way by which He reveals Himself, more rare by far, because wholly interior and spiritual. This vision is never given but to souls that seek God and desire His coming with burning desire that burns up all impurity of sin " [1]; and again he says : " When the Lord comes as a consuming fire and His Presence is understood in the power by which the soul is changed, and in the love by which it is inflamed : when all stain of sin and rust and vices have been consumed in that fire and the conscience has been purified and

[1] Canticle, tr. M. C. Patmore.

calmed, there ensues a certain sudden and unwonted enlargement of mind and an inpouring of light illuminating the intellect for the comprehension of mysteries." [1] Like the other mystics, St. Bernard teaches that purification precedes illumination, and that Love is the teacher by whose aid the soul can conquer self and sin. It is this emphasis on Love as the guide that leads him to develop the imagery of the Spiritual Marriage, so constantly found among the mediæval Christian mystics, and which is based so often on a mystical interpretation of the *Song of Solomon*. God is Love, and the soul is the Spouse of Love, who in utter self-renunciation gives herself wholly to Love, and is thereby able to discern Him Who is Love itself—to love thus is to contract marriage with God, and they who love God are one Spirit with Him.

But St. Bernard, deeply though he penetrated into the divine mysteries, was no mere visionary. He speaks of the one who has been ravished out of himself in the secret of the Divinity, and who issues out of that state on fire with the love of God and inflamed with zeal for goodness and with a great fervour for spiritual exercises ; Love, he says, is full of zeal, and zeal leads to faithful service. At twenty-five years of age St. Bernard had become Abbot of Clairvaux, and until his death he exercised a tremendous influence in the Church and upon religion generally. Though always a great contemplative, drawing his strength from his secret and continuous communion with the Divine, he yet, like so many of the great mystics, lived a life of unceasing and immense activity. He was called upon to oppose heresy, to decide between rival Popes, to preach a Crusade, to travel all over Europe on various

[1] Canticle.

missions, and withal to rule his own abbey. Yet he also found time to write. His *Sermons on the Canticle* and his treatise on *The Love of God* had a great influence on later mystical writers, and to him all who later sought to tread the Mystic Way owe a deep debt of gratitude.

Another mystical teacher of importance belonging to this period was Richard of St. Victor, who died in A.D. 1173, prior of the Abbey of St. Victor, near Paris, who was a practical reformer, striving against the abuses and formalism which had crept into monastic life, insisting on self-knowledge as the way to God and on self-purification as more important than philosophy. He holds that there are six stages of Contemplation, the first two having as their object sensible things, the second two dealing with what is beyond the senses but accessible to reason, and the last two having as their objective the unseen truth which is above reason. There is a divinely illumined eye of the soul able to search into the depths of our own nature and upward to the heights of the Divine, when it is opened " to behold God and godly things, heaven and heavenly things, and all manner of ghostly things." At such a time the soul is ravished above itself by abundance of desires and a " great multitude of love," so that it is inflamed with the light of God-head, and the earthly dies away. In this ecstasy the spirit can be joined with God and become one with Him, " when the mind of man," says Richard, " is rapt into the abyss of the Divine light, so that, utterly oblivious of all exterior things, it knows not itself and passes wholly into its God. And so in this state is held in check and lulled to deep sleep the crowd of carnal desires. In this state, while the mind is alienated from itself, while it is rapt unto the secret closet of the divine privacy, while it is on all sides encircled by the conflagration of divine love and is intimately penetrated and set on fire through and through, it strips off self and puts on a certain divine condition, and being configured to the Beauty gazed upon it passes into a new kind of glory." [1]  Union, however, must produce spiritual fruits, it is not for the mystic's mere enjoyment ; it is granted that he may bring forth fruit unto God, and in his own life the prior of St. Victor lived out that which he taught.

In St. Francis of Assisi (A.D. 1182–1226) we find a mystic of a different type from those we have just considered.  He is associated with the true Nature-Mysticism which sees the Divine life pulsating through the whole of Nature, and which holds that all living things are the children of God.  Yet in St. Francis this was combined with the strictest asceticism : unlimited love, but the uttermost humility, represented the true relation between man and God, and therefore there must be self-annihilation, and throughout his life St. Francis aimed at such a complete annihilation of his lower self as would allow the Divine Spirit to work through him unhindered. Obedience, poverty and chastity were the three vows of his order, which meant ascetism in regard to the will, to worldly possessions, and to the desires of the body, in order to secure real spiritual freedom.  But to St. Francis this was only the expression of his love, which was the ruling passion of his life, and which made his religion the joyous thing it was.  We are told in the Legend of his life how in ecstasy he would

[1] de IV. Grad. Viol. Car.

come " into a very intoxication of the divine Love,"
and in one of his prayers he says : " I beseech Thee,
O Lord, that the fiery and sweet strength of Thy
love may absorb my soul from all things that are under
heaven, that I may die for love of Thy love, as Thou
didst deign to die for love of my love." [1]  We are
told that St. Francis " yearned to be utterly transformed into God by the fire of his exceeding love."

It was by prayer that he believed the soul could attain
to contemplation and the mystic union.  His chief
study, says his biographer, was to be free from all
worldly preoccupations, lest the serenity of his mind
should be troubled, even momentarily.  So he made
himself insensible to the distraction of all outward
things, and keeping a check upon natural desires, he
would occupy himself with God alone.  It was
through the prayer of contemplation that he found the
way to Union : " In prayer," he said, " there seemeth
to be a cleansing of the inward feelings and an
union with the one true and highest Good " ; and in
his paraphrase of the Lord's Prayer, the Kingdom
to him stands for the goal of the mystic's quest, " where
there is the clear vision of Thee, the perfect love of
Thee, the blessed company of Thee, the eternal
enjoyment of Thee."

But though the life of contemplation attracted
Francis almost irresistibly, he felt that if he were to
follow his Master faithfully it must be combined with
the life of preaching and of external activity ; he held
that " to burn in contemplation and to communicate
to others the light of one's inward fire—this is perfection."  His biographer tells us how he made up his
mind in his later years that while spending a part of

[1] *Writings,* tr. P. Robinson, p. 145.

his time in the blessed retirement of contemplation, the rest must be given to the profit of his neighbour.

The influence of St. Francis did not cease with his death ; a great band of Franciscan mystics followed in his steps, among them Angela of Foligno, a great mystic who became one of the chief religious influences of her time, a teacher and director of souls, who taught her " spiritual sons " that knowledge of God and knowledge of self were the essentials and would lead to the realisation that " all goodness cometh from the Love Uncreate and not from ourselves." But the most beautiful witness to the mystical teachings of St. Francis is to be found in the writings of Jacopone da Todi, a lawyer converted in middle age, who became a leader among the spiritual Franciscans. His poems must be allowed to speak for themselves. He writes thus of the Divine Love :

> " Ineffable Love Divine
> Sweetness unformed, yet bright,
> Measureless, endless Light
> Flame in this heart of mine.
>
> It hath found the measureless way
> Itself to lose and to spend,
> And so it can comprehend
> The Immeasurable Height :
> And purifying its clay
> From all alloy or blend,
> It drinks without pause or end
> Ineffable Delight,
> Loosing—yet holding tight
> No longer the soul doth seek
> Power to tell and to speak
> Transformed so utterly." [1]

[1] *Lauda*, 91, tr. Mrs. Theodore Beck.

So purification through love enables the illumined soul to see the glory of God unveiled. Equally lovely are his verses on the Beatific Vision and the mystic Union.

> " When the mind's very being is gone,
>     Sunk in a conscious sleep,
>  In a rapture divine and deep,
>     Itself in the Godhead lost :
>  It is conquered, ravished and won !
>     Set in Eternity's sweep,
>     Gazing back on the steep,
>  Knowing not how it was crossed,
>  To a new world now it is tossed,
>     Drawn from its former state
>     To another, measureless, great.
>  Where Love is drowned in the Sea." [1]

Jacopone writes in the true Franciscan spirit, and reveals himself as one of the most fervent of the Franciscan mystics, and more than that, as a lover to whom the Vision has been granted in all its splendour, a lover who knows the joy of union consummated with the Beloved.

[1] *Lauda*, 91.

# CHAPTER VIII

# MEDIÆVAL MYSTICISM IN ENGLAND

RICHARD ROLLE of Hampole (1300–1349) is one of the earliest English mystics whose writings have come down to us. He fled the world at the age of eighteen and became a hermit, and yet, like most of the other great mystics, he found that Love drove him out of his retirement, and he went forth to preach and teach his disciples, and wrote his message that others might benefit from what he himself had received. His teaching was all of Love : " If thy life be not burning in His Love," he wrote, " little be thy delight," and his best-known work is *The Fire of Love*. He wrote also *The Amending of Life*, and other works.

The way to the amending of life was of course by way of Purgation. If we are truly to turn to God, he says, " this is naught else but to put away all lusts, to suffer all bitterness gladly for the love of God, to forgo all idle occupation and all worldly errands in so much that our soul be truly turned to God, and dieth pithily to all else. Be it enough, then, to be despised by all, but God to love, with God to be, in God to joy : from Him never to part, but to draw with desire unslaked to Him." [1] When the senses have been purged and the mind also cleansed, then the soul can see clearly the mysteries hid from those still absorbed in themselves, " for the ignorant, fleshly soul is not ravished into beholding of the Godhead, unless first it be made spiritual and all fleshly hinderings are forgone. Truly when it begins to have a clean heart and no image of bodily things beguileth it, then securely it is admitted to

[1] *The Amending of Life,* tr. Misyn, bks. 1 and 2.

high things, that in the love of God it may be wonderfully glad." [1]

To Richard Rolle God is Fire, He is Sweetness, He is Melody, and these conceptions constantly appear in his writings ; he says that he will busy himself with virtue that he may more burningly love, more sweetly sing and more deeply feel the sweetness of love. It is in the form of this imagery that he conceives of the Beatific Vision, and the union to which it leads. " When the mind now beginneth to burn in desire of its Maker, it is made able to receive uncreated light, and is so inspired and fulfilled with gifts of the Holy Ghost, so that—as far as mortals may—it is raised to the sweetness of Everlasting Life. And while the soul is filled with sweetness of the Godhead and the warmth of its Maker's light and is offered and accepted in sacrifice to the King Everlasting, it is as it were all consumed. O merry Love ! strong, ravishing, burning, wilful, unslaked, may all my soul be brought to thy service and suffered to think of nothing but thee." [2]

A lover of God and his fellows, wholly devoted and joying in his love, was this hermit of Hampole, and withal an individualist claiming the freedom of Love, who remained within the Church while yet believing that the Holy Spirit spoke to him directly and bade him speak so to others.

A mystic of this period, of whom practically nothing is known except through one little *Treatise on Contemplation*, is Margerie Kempe, the ancress of Lynn. The date at which she wrote it has been placed at *c.* 1290, and it is possible that she may have been one

[1] *The Amending of Life,* tr. Misyn, bk. 8.
[2] *Ibid.,* bk. 11.

Margery, daughter of John Kempe, of whom it is recorded that some time between 1284 and 1298 she gave up certain property to the prior and convent of Christ Church, Canterbury. From the contents of this treatise it would seem that she had been a woman of wealth and social position who abandoned the world in order to become an anchoress.

This treatise is evidently only a fragment of a complete book of hers, and it represents Christ's words to this lover of His. " Daughter," He says, " thou mayst no better please God than to think continually in His love" [1]; and again : " Daughter, if thou wear the habergeon or the hair (shirt), fasting bread and water, and if thou saidest every day a thousand Pater Nosters, thou shalt not please Me so well as thou dost when thou art in silence and suffrest Me to speak in thy soul." [2] To Margerie Kempe, as might be expected from an anchoress, the contemplative life, spent in mediation and prayer, seemed the highest type : " Thinking, weeping, and high contemplation is the best life in earth." [3] So great was her love to her Lord and so constant her meditation upon Him that the sight of suffering, whatever it might be, to her represented His Passion, and " her mind was all ravished in to our Lord Jesu." To her, heaven was the presence of her Lord, and were He in hell, it would become heaven to her. " I would liefer be there (in hell)," she says, " as long as Thou wouldest and please Thee, than to be in this world and displease Thee." [4] Through suffering and humility and shame she sought to follow in the steps of her Lord, and she had His consoling

---

[1] *Cell of Self-Knowledge*, p. 51.       [2] *Ibid.*, p. 52.
[3] *Ibid.*, p. 53.                       [4] *Ibid.*, p. 54.

assurance that this was the right way to heaven, and that only by this means might she attain, as many wiser and greater than herself might never attain, to the perfect love of God.

Another mystic of this period of whom nothing is known except from his writings is the author of *The Cloud of Unknowing* and several other works, including the *Dionise Hid Divinitie*, the first English translation of the *Mystical Theology* of Dionysius the " Areopagite." This writer was evidently a mystic himself, and a great contemplative who loved solitude and silence, but he seems also to have been a spiritual director of experience in guiding souls along the Mystic Way. He teaches that God is beyond the reach of human understanding and can be found only by the soul which, in its love and desire for Him, has passed beyond knowing and entered the " cloud of unknowing." Man may have knowledge and be able to think of all creatures, " but of God Himself can no man think—He may well be loved but not thought. By love may He be gotten and holden ; but by thought never. Though it be good some time to think of the kindness of God, and although it be a light and a part of contemplation, nevertheless yet in this work it shall be cast down and covered with a cloud of forgetting. And thou shalt step above it with a devout and a pleasing stirring of love and try for to pierce that darkness above thee. And smite upon that thick cloud of unknowing with a sharp dart of longing love ; and go not thence for thing that befalleth." [1]

The substance of all perfection is nothing but a good will, says the writer, a will which is in conformity

[1] *The Cloud of Unknowing,* chap. 6.

with the Divine Will. " Mean God all and all God, so that nought work in thy wit and in thy will, but only God." [1] He describes the mystical experience with a clearness which can come only from his own first-hand knowledge. It is the result of a good will, " a swift piercing act, an act of direction, a naked intent of the will fastening itself upon God," but as we have seen above, this act of direction is motived by love, " that sharp dart of longing love," which is directed towards God, and in the joy that comes of loving Him the soul ceases to have knowledge or feeling of its own. Only the soul which has " noughted " and unclothed itself can hope to be " clothed with the gracious feeling of God Himself."

Though this writer speaks of the mystic experience as a state in which the soul is rapt away from the bodily senses, and to him the spiritual has nothing to do with the phenomenal, " nowhere bodily is everywhere spiritually," yet he teaches no doctrine of passivity or quietism. The mystic needs to be up and doing and ever striving towards his end : " Look now forwards," says this wise counsellor, " and let be backwards."

A mystical writer of a different type from the author of *The Cloud of Unknowing* was Walter Hilton or Hylton, Canon of Thurgarton Priory near Southwell, who died in 1396. Though there is little doubt that his mystical teaching is based on his own spiritual experiences, he gives no account of these ; he was evidently not so much a contemplative as a director of souls, and his writings are directed towards the end of helping others in their spiritual life. His best-known work is *The Scale of Perfection*, in which

[1] *The Cloud of Unknowing*, chap. 40.

he traces the steps by which the earnest seeker may attain to perfection. " The contemplative life," he writes, " lieth in perfect love and charity felt inwardly by spiritual virtues and by truthful knowing and sight of God and spiritual things." [1] The first part of contemplation is knowledge of God, the second is affection, that is, loving devotion, without knowledge of spiritual things, and the third consists in both knowing and perfect loving of God. This means illumination joined to a " soft, sweet, burning love," by which the soul is ravished unto union for a brief time, though this cannot be enjoyed in fullness until the soul reaches the bliss of heaven.

The soul of man is made in the image of God, and " in the first shaping was wonderfully bright and fair, full of burning love and spiritual light," [2] but it has become foul and encrusted with sin. Perfection can only be attained by the reform of the soul, which can be accomplished in part in this world and in full at the last. The way of reform is hard and long, but by much travail the seeker may come thereto, " when he is first healed of his spiritual sickness, and when all bitter passions and fleshly lusts and old feelings are burned out of the heart with fire of desire and new gracious feelings are brought in with burning love and spiritual light." [3]

When the soul has come to know itself and is cleansed from its sins and forgets itself in burning love to God, then He grants to it the Vision of Himself : " He openeth the inner eyes of the soul when He lighteneth the reason through touching and shining of His blessed light, for to see Him and know Him ; not all

[1] *The Scale of Perfection*, i. 3.
[2] *Ibid.*, ii. 1.          [3] *Ibid.*, ii. 17.

at once but by divers times, and by that sight He
ravisheth all the affection of the soul to Him. And
then beginneth the soul for to know Him spiritually
and burningly for to love Him." [1]

The end and purpose of attaining perfection is the
union of the soul with God in perfect love, and of this
Hilton tells us in his *Song of Angels*. This union or
" onehead," he writes, " is verily made when the
mights of the soul are reformed by grace to the dignity
and the state of the first condition, when the mind
is established firmly without changing and vagation
in God and spiritual things, and when the reason
is cleared from all worldly and fleshly beholdings
and from all bodily imagination, figures and fantasies
of creatures, and is illumined by grace to behold
God and spiritual things, and when the will and the
affection is purified and cleansed from all fleshly,
kindly and worldly love and is inflamed with burning
love of the Holy Spirit." [2]   This union means partaking of the Divine qualities, and therefore the soul thus
closely united with its Lord will be possessed of
power and wisdom and holiness and peace. " Much
comfort it receiveth of our Lord, not only inwardly
in its secret nature, by virtue of the onehead to our
Lord that lieth in knowing and loving of God, in
light and spiritual burning of Him, in transforming of
the soul in to the Godhead," [3] but also in its relation
to all outward things, for the soul thus living the
unitive life looks with a new eye upon the universe :
it sees, hears and feels only God in all creatures.

But Walter Hilton knew that life does not consist
in raptures and visions, and he closes his treatise with

---

[1] *The Scale of Perfection*, ii. 32 ; ii. 34.
[2] *The Cell of Self-Knowledge*, pp. 63–64.        [3] *Ibid.*, p. 65.

a caution not to depend too much on these and adds :
" It sufficeth to me for to live in truth and in faith
principally, and not in feeling."

The last, but by no means the least important, of
the English mediæval mystics to be considered in this
chapter is Julian of Norwich (1343–after 1413), an
anchoress who was granted a series of visions when
she was about thirty years old, and who wrote an
account of them in her *Revelations of Divine Love.*
She is one of the most philosophic of the early English
mystics, and her mystical views seem in part to be
based on Plato.  To her the only revelation of God
that could be possible was the vision of Him as Love.
She says concerning His nature that, " He is to us
everything that is good and comfortable for us : He
is our clothing that for love wrappeth us, claspeth us
and all encloseth us for tender love, that He may never
leave us ;  being to us all thing that is good—the blissful Godhead—Almighty, All-Wisdom, All-Love. He
that made all things for love, by the same love keepeth
them and shall keep them without end." [1]

She tells how God revealed to her that He was the
Might and the Goodness of the Fatherhood, the
Wisdom of the Motherhood, the Light and the Grace
that is all blessed Love, the Trinity, the Unity, the
sovereign Goodness of all manner of things, the One
that maketh to love and to long, and the endless
fulfilling of all true desires.  In every vision she
says that she perceived three properties of God :
Life, Love and Light.

She regards the soul as of one nature with God,
and therefore it can become one with Him : " Thus
is the Nature-made rightfully oned to the maker,

[1] *Revelations of Divine Love,* chaps. 5, 8.

which is substantial Nature not-made, that is God.
And therefore it is that there may nor shall be right
naught between God and man's soul." [1]  Through
prayer the human will can be made one with the Divine
Will and man attains to likeness to God. " Beseeching
is a true, gracious, lasting will of the soul, oned and
fastened into the will of our Lord—our Lord willeth
to have our prayer, because with His grace He maketh
us like to Himself in condition as we are in kind." [2]
Prayer becomes desire to behold, and that in its turn
becomes a high and mighty desire to be all oned unto
Him, centred to His dwelling.  The Vision of God
was to Julian a reality granted in this life to the
mystic : " The beholding of this while we are here,"
she says, " is full pleasing to God and full great
profit to us : and the soul that thus beholdeth
maketh it like to Him that is beheld and oneth it in
rest and peace by His grace." [3]

And what was the Lord's meaning in thus giving
to Julian these revelations of Himself ?  The answer
came to her spirit saying : " Wouldst thou learn thy
Lord's meaning in this thing ?  Learn it well : Love
was His meaning.  Who shewed it thee ?  Love.
What shewed He thee ?  Love.  Wherefore shewed
it He ?  For Love.  Hold thee therein, and thou
shalt learn and know more in the same." [4]

In the last words of her book, Julian fitly sums up
her mystical doctrine concerning God and His
relation to man.

" And I saw full surely that ere God made us He
loved us ; which love was never slacked nor ever shall
be.  And in this love He hath done all His works,

---

[1] *Revelations of Divine Love*, chap. 53.
[2] *Ibid.*, chap. 41.    [3] *Ibid.*, chap. 68.    [4] *Ibid.*, chap. 86.

and in this love He hath made all things profitable to us, and in this love our life is everlasting. In our making we had beginning; but the love wherein He made us was in Him from without beginning, in which love we have our beginning. And all this shall we see in God, without end."

# CHAPTER IX

# GERMAN AND FLEMISH MYSTICISM

The development of Mysticism in Germany and Flanders is notable for the number of women mystics who contributed to the movement, among them St. Hildegarde (1098–1179), the German abbess and prophetess, who conceived of God under the image of the " Living Light," and whose writings give her a place among the mystics ; Mechthild of Magdeburg (1210–1285), whose teaching was very influential in her time, and whose book, *The Effulgence of Divine Light*, formed a mystic classic, and St. Gertrude the Great (1256–1301). These women and others like them added to their mysticism and their asceticism a reforming zeal which was much needed in their time, and they led the way in the quest for a higher ideal of religion within the Church.

But the first of those who tried to formulate a philosophy which should embody a more spiritual ideal of religion in accordance with the doctrines of the Church was Eckhart (1260–1327), a great speculative mystic and a member of the Dominican order. He distinguishes between God, the Divine Power at work within the universe, and the Godhead, " all that is in the Godhead is One—above all names, above all nature. God works, so doth not the Godhead.—The end of all things is the hidden Darkness of the eternal Godhead, unknown and never to be known." [1] God is the " uttered word " of the Godhead, Who beholds Himself in an Eternal Now. Eckhart holds that there is within the soul a divine Spark, which rejects all creatures and seeks God alone, since

---

[1] *Pfeiffer*, p. 173.

its return to That whence it came is its salvation. Being, that is, the Divine, he identifies with Good, and evil is therefore not-being. It follows that purity is essential for the soul that seeks union with its Source, for God will dwell nowhere save in a pure soul : as the eye can endure no foreign substance within it, so the pure soul can endure nothing in itself, no stain which may come between it and God. " Love separates all things from the soul. She suffers nought to come near her that is not God nor God-like." When the soul has thus been purified, she finds God within herself, as she pours herself out into the " supernatural of the pure Godhead," and so she is one with God and He with her. But Eckhart defends himself against the pantheism of which he has not unnaturally been accused ; the soul and God are not completely one in nature, and he asks, " How stands it with the soul that is lost in God ? Does the soul find herself or not ? It appears to me that the soul finds herself in the point where every rational being understands itself with itself. Although it sinks and sinks in the eternity of the Divine Essence, yet it can never reach the ground. Therefore God has left a little point wherein the soul turns back upon itself and knows itself to be a creature."

Eckhart preached boldly a spiritual mysticism which was too much at variance with the dogmas of the Church to pass unnoticed, and the Pope condemned him for heresy, but his preaching had borne fruit, and it was his followers who became the leaders of the movement embodied in the society of the " Friends of God," which was influenced also by the writings of the great women saints already mentioned. The movement arose mainly as the result of the troublous times through which Europe was passing, when wars and famine and pestilence turned men's minds to inner things ; the " Friends of God," who included men and women of every rank and state, were a body of sincere Christians who were concerned with the better tending of the inner life, and who strove to live in accordance with the law of universal love.

One of the greatest of these Friends of God was Tauler (1300–1361), also a Dominican and a great preacher. In most respects his doctrine agrees with that of his master Eckhart. He lays stress on the transcendence of God, the Unity in which all multiplicity is transcended, Who is Being and becoming, rest and motion. He also emphasises the fact of God's indwelling in the soul, saying : " God hath impressed on us his image and superscription in the inmost inmost of the soul. Thus is the inmost of our soul united to the inmost of the very Godhead." The hindrance to true union is sin, and the essence of sin is self-assertion and self-will ; therefore the soul must die to self and to such death " eternal life answers." The stages of this dying to self mean self-control, imitation of Christ in conformity to the Divine will, and finally the giving up of all that is external, and complete submission into the hands of God.

Thus purified, the soul will find its whole and only satisfaction in God, will relish and desire nothing but God, and its thoughts and intents will be ever occupied with God. Then, when " the outward man has been converted into the inward, reasonable man, and the powers of the senses and the powers of the reason are gathered up into the very centre of the man's being—the unseen depths of his spirit, wherein lies the image of God—and thus he flings himself into the Divine abyss, in which he dwelt eternally before he was created ; then the Godhead bends down and descends into the depths of the pure, waiting soul, and transforms the created soul, drawing it up into the uncreated essence, so that the spirit becomes one with Him." [1]

Again he says that the spirit is received and utterly swallowed up in the Abyss which is its source, and then transcends itself and all its powers, and mounts higher and higher towards the Divine Dark, even as an eagle towards the sun.  When the created spirit has lost itself in the Spirit of God, then " the sole Unity, which is God, answers truly to the oneness of the soul, for then is there nothing in the soul beside God." [2]

Yet with all his deep philosophic mysticism, Tauler was an energetic priest, performing all his pastoral duties faithfully and zealously.  He held that spiritual enjoyments were the food of the soul, and therefore only to be taken as nourishment and support to help us forward in our active work ; mysticism was to have its fruits in ordinary human life.

A mystic of a different type from the practical Tauler was Henry Suso (? 1295–1365), a saint and a poet, who wrote of himself as the " Servitor " of the Divine Wisdom, for it was as Wisdom, Eternal and Uncreate, that he conceived of Reality.  This is the Source and Eternal beginning of all things, and therefore God can be seen as He is mirrored in His works.  In a long description of the beauties of the

[1] Sermon for the 15th Sunday after Trinity.
[2] Sermon for the 23rd Sunday after Trinity.

natural world, Suso breaks off to exclaim : " Ah, gentle God, if Thou art so lovely in Thy creatures, how exceeding beautiful and ravishing Thou must be in Thyself ! " [1]

There is, he holds, an image of God in the soul, which can rise to the Divine Essence or Source, but this can only be attained by perfect detachment ; the first stage of this is to turn away from the world and the lusts thereof, the second is patient endurance of all that befalls us, and the third is imitation of Christ. Suso subjected himself to terrible self-torture and indescribable austerities in order to subdue his body and spirit, and to share in the suffering of Christ, and this he did for many years, till it was revealed to him that he should cease from these mortifications of himself. He says that all the powers have one object and one work, and this is to be conformed to the eternal Truth ; the spiritual man must bring his body into subjection to his spirit—he himself knew something of this—and everything done should be directed to the end of discovering the super-essential Spirit and laying hold of It. When the soul has been purified, then it must withdraw itself into a profound stillness, and having reached spiritual perfection, it can pass beyond time and space : " The spirit, spiritualising itself, soars up, now flying on the summitless heights, now swimming in the bottomless depths of the sublime marvels of the Godhead." [2] Here the spirit arrives at the Nought of the Unity, it enters into God, and is lost in the still-ness of the glorious, dazzling darkness, and of the naked simple Unity. " Here the Divine Nature doth, as it were, embrace the soul—that they may be

---

[1] *Life*, tr. T. F. Knox, p. 225.    [2] *Ibid.*, p. 242.

for ever one. He who is thus received into the Eternal Nothing is in the Everlasting Now and hath neither before nor after." [1]

Suso, though life brought him many trials and undeserved persecution, was always at the service of others, even when his help was given at great cost to himself ; his saintliness won him much affection and regard, and caused many to seek him out as their confessor and spiritual guide, notably the " spiritual daughter " to whom he wrote the description of the relation of the soul to God, and the final attainment of the mystic union, given above. He also, like Tauler, held that " spiritual enjoyments," the visions given to him, were given only that they might bear fruit in service to others.

We come now to one of the greatest mystics of the Catholic Church, the Fleming, John of Ruysbroeck (1293–1381), who concerns himself not so much with speculation as with the means by which the God-seeking man can attain to the mystic union. The first stage of the way is the active life, the practice of the virtues ; the second is the inward life, in which we shall follow the splendour of God, back into that source whence it comes forth, and there we shall feel our spirits stripped of all things, and we shall sink down, without thought of rising, into the pure and fathomless ocean of love. The third stage, to which few attain, is the contemplative life, in which those who are perfectly purified are one with the Divine brightness, and they are transformed and made one with that Light which they see, and through which they see. " What we are, that we behold : and what we behold, that we are ; for in this pure

[1] Vaughan, *Hours with the Mystics*, p. 270.

vision we are one life and one spirit with God. This possession is a simple and abysmal tasting of all good and eternal life, and in this tasting we are swallowed up above reason, and without reason, in the deep Quiet of the Godhead, which is never moved." [1] Those who experience this, says Ruysbroeck, who was one of them, are one being and one life and one blessedness with God.

But that one who has consummated the union with the Divine must bear fruit to God of that union. In the last chapter of his *Book of the Sparkling Stone*, Ruysbroeck tells of what nature this fruit should be. " The man who is sent down by God from these heights into the world is full of truth and rich in all virtues. And he seeks not his own, but the glory of Him Who has sent him ; therefore he must always spend himself on those who have need of him—he possesses a universal life, for he is ready alike for contemplation and for action and is perfect in both of them." [2]

Ruysbroeck himself did the work of a cathedral priest till he was fifty years old, and when he withdrew to a community life, it was to busy himself with teaching and writing—some dozen of his books have come down to us. There, too, he lived the life of true brotherhood, ready to serve all who needed his service, seeking to carry his own precepts into practice and to live the " universal life."

The last development of German mysticism which we have space to consider is the little treatise called the *Theologia Germanica*, by an unknown writer, a book of devotion based on the teachings of Eckhart.

[1] *Book of the Sparkling Stone*, tr. Wynschenk Dom, p. 204.
[2] *Ibid.*, p. 221.

Emphasis is laid by the writer on self-renunciation and the annihilation of the will in the mystic who seeks to come to God and to be illuminated by the Divine Light. " Behold, in such a man," he says, " must all thoughts of Self, all self-seeking, self-will and what cometh thereof, be utterly lost and surrendered and given over to God ; and whatever cometh to pass in a man who is truly Godlike, whether he do or suffer, all is done in this Light and this Love ; and in his heart there is a content and a quietness, so that he does not desire to know more or less, to have, to live, to die, to be or not to be— these become all one and alike to him and he complaineth of nothing but of sin only : and sin is to desire or will anything otherwise than the One Perfect Good and the One Eternal Will ; all that we call sin cometh hence, that man hath another will than God and the True Good ; for were there no will but the One Will, no sin could ever be committed." [1]

Then, when a man has forsaken and come out of himself, God can enter in, and God and man can be wholly united. " To be a partaker of the Divine Nature means to be illuminated by the Divine Light and to be inflamed and consumed with Divine Love " ; man so gives place to God that God Himself is there and the two work as one ; man lives in, and through, and for God alone.

[1] Tr. S. Winkworth, p. 154.

# CHAPTER X

# MYSTICISM IN ITALY AND SPAIN

IT was not only in Germany and Flanders that the movement towards Mysticism developed within the Catholic Church. We find the same thing in Italy, where the movement had as its leaders two great saints and mystics, Catherine of Siena (1347–1380) and Catherine of Genoa (1447–1510).

The former was born at a time of great corruption and turmoil, when the Italian cities were in open rebellion against their spiritual head, and the Pope was an exile at Avignon. Catherine early shewed signs of the spiritual greatness to which she was to attain ; even as a child she had visions, and at six years old she started out to find a solitary place wherein to live the life of the desert hermits. At sixteen she devoted herself to the religious life, as a recluse in her father's house, and shortly afterwards she became a member of the Third Order of St. Dominic, spending her life in austerities and prayer and ecstasy. In 1366 she had a vision of Christ, Who in the presence of all the company of Heaven espoused her to Himself, and bade her " act courageously," and this command of her Heavenly Spouse she fulfilled to the end of her life.

She came out from her seclusion and gave herself to the work of nursing the sick, but presently found herself called upon to take her part in bringing peace to Italy. She was devoted to her Church and grieved at the corruptions within it and the evil lives of many of the clergy, and she called boldly upon the Pope to reform them. She also urged him in the strongest terms to return to Rome, and herself took an active share in reconciling the cities which were hostile to the Holy See. She was possessed of a statesmanlike ability for dealing with public affairs, and for a period she was one of the chief political powers of her time ; yet with all her work for Church and State she found time for the care of souls and for work among the poor, for the " universal life," lived in God and for man.

The Way, for her too, had been the Purgative life, lived in those years of seclusion at home ; we find in her writings this account of it : " What soever he be that cometh to the service of God, if he will have God truly, it is needful to him that he make his heart naked from all sensible love, not only of certain persons, of every creature what that ever be, and then he should stretch up his soul to our Lord and Maker, simply, with all the desire of his heart. For an heart may not wholly be given to God, but if it be free from all other love, open and simple, without doubleness." [1]

Such self-stripping was possible only through love : " The soul is a tree existing by love," said Catherine, " and can live by nothing else but love. Needs be, then, that the root of this tree should grow in and issue from the circle of true self-knowledge, which is contained in God, Who has neither beginning nor end."

By purification and self-knowledge the soul could be fitted for the unitive life, lived in and for God. " A soul which is verily united to God," wrote Catherine, who was living that life of union, " perceiveth not, seeth not, nor loveth not herself, nor none other soul, nor hath no mind of no creature, but only on God. And of this unity of love that is increased every day in such a soul, she is transformed

[1] *Cell of Self-Knowledge,* p. 45.

in a manner in to our Lord, that she may neither think nor understand nor love, nor have no mind but God or else in God." [1]

St. Catherine of Siena was but thirty-three when she died, but she had been true to her troth, she had lived courageously, and had proved herself to be one of the great leaders and saints of the Church.

Of a different type, and called to a different sphere, was her great namesake, St. Catherine of Genoa. This Catherine was of aristocratic birth, and married, living the life of her class and state till she was converted at the age of twenty-seven, when " her heart was pierced by a sudden and immense love of God, and in a transport of pure and all-purifying love, she was drawn away from all the miseries of the world." She devoted herself to work among the sick, and also to religious discipline, and a little later founded the first hospital in Genoa. For over twenty years she lived a life of active service for God, and a life of the closest communion with Him. It was in the closing years of her life, when failing health limited her activities, that she formulated her mystical doctrine, based on her own direct, personal experience.

Her conception of God is made plain by the names which she uses in her teaching ; He is to her Sun, Light, Fire—we shall see in her doctrine of Purification how she thinks of Him as a consuming Fire—He is Air and Ocean ; Beauty, Truth, Love, Goodness. It was her craving for unification which made her conceive of the " one true divine root-centre " of her individual soul as present everywhere ; the glorious God, to her, is the essence of things both visible and invisible.

[1] *Cell of Self-Knowledge*, p. 38.

Catherine has much to teach of purification, not only in this world, but as it is completed after death, which becomes a doctrine of Purgatory. She says that when the soul has consumed all the evil inclinations of the body, God consumes all the imperfections of the soul. The soul after death, when it finds itself to be impure, seeks Purgatory, and casts itself in, because of the " impetuosity of that love which exists between God and the soul, and tends to conform the soul to God." Then the Divine Fire consumes every imperfection in the soul, and the soul thus purified abides altogether in God without stain, and its being is in God.

Of the love which inspires this passion for purity and union, Catherine says : " The love of God is our true self-love, since these selves of ours were created by and for Love Itself " ; and again : " Pure love loves God without why or wherefore. The soul offers and remits itself entirely to Him, so that it can no more operate except in the manner willed by tender Love Himself ; and henceforth it does not produce works except such as are pure, full and sincere, works that please God-Love." [1]

Her sense of unification, and her own love for God, expressed themselves in a passionate longing for union with Eternal Love ; Love cannot be quiet until it has arrived at its ultimate perfection. " Love," she cries, " I want Thee, the whole of Thee " ; and again she says that the spirit is ever longing to be free from all bodily sensations, so that it may be able to unite itself to God through love. In Catherine's descriptions of attainment to the mystic union, her tendency to pantheism leads her also to the doctrine

[1] Cf. von Hügel, *Mystical Element in Religion,* i, p. 268.

of deification. "The Divine Love," she says, "is the very God, infused by His own immense Goodness into our hearts. . . . My Being is God, not by simple participation, but by a true transformation of my Being—God is my Being, my Me, my Strength, my Beatitude, my Good, my Delight."[1]

It was by the self-chosen life of asceticism that Catherine attained to the union she sought, and it was by that unitive life as contemplative and mystic that she was enabled to live her life in the world, a life given up not to active service only, but to constant spiritual teaching to the many disciples who gathered round her.

Spanish mysticism reached its greatest heights in the sixteenth century, and we find in it an austerity and a severity very different from the freedom of the movement in Germany and Italy; but in Spain the mystics lived ever under the shadow of the Inquisition, there was no place for any development not approved by Holy Church. St. Ignatius Loyola was typical of the movement. He was born towards the end of the fifteenth century, and his youth was given up to a life of pleasure, but after being wounded in 1521 he was converted and went into retreat. There he prepared himself for his great task, the foundation of the Society of Jesus, formed to carry on the work of rescue and sanctification for which Jesus Christ had come to earth. He was a true representative of the Church Militant, but he was also a saint who had trodden the Mystic Way, and he sets forth the training required for the soul in his *Spiritual Exercises*.

The great mystic St. Teresa (1515–1582) owed much to his teaching and to the spiritual influence of

[1] Cf. von Hügel, *Mystical Element in Religion*, i, pp. 260 ff.

his Order. To her we owe one of the clearest and most complete descriptions of the mystic experiences of a saint. She was of noble birth, and this fact no doubt helped her to become the able administrator and ruler of her later days. She early gave herself to the religious life as a Carmelite nun at Avila, but she found that it was possible to have as many temptations and to lead as easy a life in seclusion as in the life of the world. At last, in 1562, she was enabled to found the first reformed Carmelite convent, under the primitive rules of the Order, and she spent the rest of her life in raising the spiritual level of the Carmelite convents and in the care and education of souls, and especially her own nuns. To this end she wrote her own *Life*, and also *The Interior Castle*, a treatise on Prayer, and the *Way of Perfection*.

St. Teresa is famed for her teaching on Prayer, which she divides into four stages : the first that of mental prayer, which costs the soul much labour in withdrawing itself from outward distractions ; the second that of the prayer of quiet, in which the soul begins to retire within itself, and the will is given over to God. This prayer is but a spark of the Divine Love, lit by God in the soul, which is later to kindle the burning, flaming fire of the Love of God. The third stage is the prayer of union, in which the soul is no longer her own, but abides entirely in God; the last stage is the " spiritual marriage," when the soul receives an illumination which shines on the spirit like a most dazzling cloud of light. Now, says the saint, " all sensation is lost in joy, which the soul is not able to understand. It is a flight the spirit takes above itself and all created things, a sweet, delicious and noiseless flight."

In *The Interior Castle* St. Teresa tells how the soul must be prepared, passing from one mansion to another, till in the innermost of all, the mystic marriage can be consummated. There must first be asceticism and self-discipline—Teresa spent much of her life in securing this—and this must take the form of complete conformity to the Will of God. She speaks of it thus in her *Life* : " The soul now seeks not and possesses not any other will but that of doing our Lord's Will, and so it prays Him to let it be so ; it gives to Him the keys of its own will. The soul will do nothing but the will of our Lord, for from henceforth the soul will have nothing of its own— all it seeks is to do everything for His glory and according to His will." [1]

Of the fact of union for the soul which thus surrenders itself wholly to God, St. Teresa has no doubts ; she had experienced it so truly herself. " The soul neither sees, hears nor understands while she is united to God—God establishes Himself in the interior of this soul in such a way that, when she comes to herself, it is impossible for her to doubt that she has been in God and God in her. So does that Beauty and Majesty remain stamped on the soul that nothing can drive it from her memory. The soul is no longer the same, always enraptured."

Teresa warns her readers against supposing that the " spiritual marriage " leads only to present enjoyment. It must and will lead to fruition. The soul which becomes one with Perfect Goodness by the high union of spirit with Spirit, shares the Divine strength, and applies herself with greater ardour than before to all that belongs to the service of God, while still

[1] *Life*, tr. Lewis, p. 154.

at times enjoying that mystic communion. " Work,
work," was St. Teresa's motto, and it was the inner
flame that inspired her to the life of outward service
and enabled her to keep the balance between the
contemplative and the active life which made her the
great saint and religious leader that she was.

Well might the poet Crashaw, himself a mystic,
write of her :

> " O thou undaunted daughter of desires !
> By all thy dower of Lights and Fires ;
> By all the eagle in thee, all the dove ;
> By all thy lives and deaths of love ;
> By thy large draughts of intellectual day,
> And by thy thirsts of love more large than they ;
> By all thy brim-fill'd Bowls of fierce desire,
> By thy last Morning's draught of liquid fire ;
> By the full kingdom of that final kiss
> That seized thy parting Soul and seal'd thee His ;
> By all the heav'ns thou hast in Him,
> (Fair sister of the Seraphim)
> By all of Him we have in Thee ;
> Leave nothing of my Self in me.
> Let me so read thy life, that I
> Unto all life of mine may die."

St. John of the Cross (1542–1591) was a disciple
of St. Teresa, and followed in her steps in his militant
work for the reform of the Carmelite monasteries.
For his reforming zeal he suffered imprisonment for
eight months at the hands of those who were opposed
to reform. He taught that all our effort should lead
up to union with God, and to attain that there must be
entire stripping away of all else, utter renunciation,
complete self-abandonment.

In his *Spiritual Canticle* and *The Living Flame of
Love*, St. John sets forth his mystical doctrine. He
holds that God is present in the inmost being of the

soul, that there is an awakening of God in the soul, and in the soul a consciousness of the divine life stirring within it. Then is felt the Touch of God, and the will " burns with the fire of love, longs for God and prays to Him in the sweetness of love." Now the soul is prepared to undertake the journey on the way to Union, and in the *Ascent of Mount Carmel* and the *Obscure Night of the Soul* St. John speaks of the stages of the way. The point of departure is the privation of all desire and complete detachment from the world : the road is by faith, and faith means night to the intellect, to which the divine goal is incomprehensible. There can be no love of God until there is detachment from all desire save that of following Him. The night of the senses and of the mind is followed by the night of the soul, when it sinks into oblivion, and God humbles and purifies it that it may be transformed in union with Himself : " That union and transformation of the soul in God," writes St. John, " which is only then accomplished when there subsists the likeness which love begets— this union—takes effect when two wills, the will of God and the will of the soul, are conformed together. Thus the soul, when it shall have driven away from itself all that is contrary to the Divine Will, becomes transformed in God by Love." [1]

He has some beautiful things to say of this passionate love : " Love has set the soul on fire, and transmuted it into love, has annihilated and destroyed it as to all that is not love. The soul on fire with love to God longs for the perfection and consummation of its love, that it may be completely refreshed." [2]

[1] *Ascent of Mount Carmel*, tr. Lewis, p. 77.
[2] *Spiritual Canticle*, ix. 7 ; xxvi. 18.

So the soul prays that God will grant it the vision of Himself, even though the vision and His Beauty mean that it dies to itself, for " the soul knows well that in the instant of that vision it will be itself absorbed and transformed into that Beauty, and be made beautiful like it." But union to St. John means more than transformation into the likeness of God, it means deification ; in that perfect union God " penetrates " the soul, " deifies " the very substance of it, and so it becomes divine, and, by participation, God.

It is plain that St. John wrote of that which he had himself experienced. It was not without reason that he was called St. John of the Cross ; he had borne his cross unflinchingly, and so at the last he won his crown, the attainment of the mystic's quest, the goal of all his efforts, that perfect union of the loving soul with the God she loved.

# CHAPTER XI

# MODERN MYSTICISM

THE development of Mysticism in Spain and the writings of St. Teresa had a considerable influence in France, where Mysticism became a living force in the Church in the seventeenth and eighteenth centuries. French mysticism was by no means so austere as the movement in Spain, nor as philosophical in character as the movement in Germany; it was deeply tinged by sentiment, though none the less genuine for that. The leaders in France were as often drawn from the laity as from the Church itself, and the general tendency of the movement was towards Quietism, which brought upon it the condemnation of the Church.

The mystics produced by this development include some great names in the history of the Catholic Church, among them Madame Acarie (1566–1618), who was responsible for the establishment of Carmelite convents, after the pattern of St. Teresa's foundations in France; her "spiritual son," St. Francis de Sales (1567–1622), who has left us a fine description of contemplative prayer in his *Treatise on the Love of God*, and who led many to seek to find God by the Mystic Way; St. Vincent de Paul (1581–1660), whose mysticism led him to a life of practical good works, for which his name will be known as long as the Catholic Church survives; Pascal (1623–1662), to whom the mystical experience was granted "in the flash of a single moment," and who was led thereby to turn his back on the world and to give himself wholly to God; and Brother Lawrence (1610–1691), the Carmelite lay-brother, who could practise the Presence of God even while occupied with all the menial duties of his station.

To this group, too, belong two English mystics, who learnt much of their mysticism in France. One of these was the Benedictine Augustine Baker (1575–1641), who in his book of *Holy Wisdom* wrote concerning prayer, and the union, to attain which prayer was the means. He taught that the soul reached the mystic union in that portion of it which is visible to God only and which He alone can inhabit : " the summit of the mind, the fund and centre of the spirit, the essence of the soul." The other was his pupil Dame Gertrude More (1606–1633), who taught once more the doctrine of mystical love. In her *Spiritual Exercises* she writes : " O let me sit alone, silent to all the world, and it to me, that I may learn the song of love " ; and again she prays : " O my God, let me walk in the way of love which knoweth not how to seek self in anything whatsoever. O sight to be wished, desired and longed for, because once to have seen Thee is to have learned all things ! Nothing can bring us to this sight but love. O Lord, give this love into my soul, that I may never more live nor breathe, but out of a most pure love of Thee, my all and only Good."

This doctrine of disinterested love formed the main part of the teaching of the French Quietists, of whom the chief were Madame Guyon (1648–1717), and Fénelon, her friend and supporter. Madame Guyon, married at sixteen to a man much her senior, whose mother tyrannised over the young wife, and made her married life thoroughly unhappy, was shewn the way to Mysticism by a Franciscan recluse whom she had consulted concerning her spiritual state. From that time prayer and devotion became the chief joys of her life, and in spite of the persecution of her husband and mother-in-law, she lived a life of spiritual happiness, upheld by the constant sense of union. After her husband's death, she led an active life of service to others, occupying herself in the founding of hospitals and in constant teaching and correspondence. She became suspected of heresy, and suffered imprisonment and much harsh treatment.

Her writings give a careful analysis of her spiritual states, and shew plainly her faith in Quietism, in the doctrine of disinterested love, and in the result for the soul which, inspired by love, surrenders itself wholly into the hands of God, and so becomes deified. She says of herself that the Well-Beloved was the only object which attracted her heart wholly to Himself, and that in losing all the gifts, she had found the Giver. Of the mystic experience she writes : " Now He alone appeared to me, my soul having given up its place to Him. It seemed to me as if it was wholly and altogether passed into its God, to make but one and the same thing with Him—I could seem to see and know God only and not myself. It was thus that my soul was lost in God, Who communicated to it His qualities." Her life of patient endurance under the afflictions which she suffered is the best testimony to the sincerity of her convictions, and the reality of that inward union.

Madame Guyon was not the only victim of the Church's persecution of Quietism. The Spanish priest Molinos (1640–1697) paid with his life for his quietist mysticism. In his *Spiritual Guide* he pointed the way to the knowledge of God by the " exterior " way of meditation and the " interior " road of contemplation, which aim at union with God by means of complete renunciation of the personal will and surrender to the Divine Will. " Wouldst thou that the omnipotent King should enter into thy soul ? " he asks. " Thou must see to it that thy heart be pure, innocent, quiet and free, unoccupied and empty, silent and meek, innocent of sins and shortcomings, free from fear, emptied of all thought." In another passage he describes the whole of the mystical progress, from Purgation to Union, which to him means deification : " The Soul that would be perfect begins to mortify its passions, and when 'tis advanced in that exercise, it denies itself, then, with the Divine Aid, it passes to the state of Nothing. This Annihilation, to make it perfect in the Soul, must be in a man's own Judgment, in his Will, in his Works, Inclinations, Desires, Thoughts and in itself ; so that the soul must find itself dead. O what a happy Soul is that which is thus dead and annihilated ! It lives no longer in itself, because God lives in it, and now it may most truly be said of it, that it is—changed, spiritualised, transformed and deified." [1]

Molinos had need of his mystic faith, for the Inquisition was not prepared to tolerate such heresy ; he was condemned, and sent to a dungeon and death. Fénelon was yet another who had to suffer for his mystical views. It was after the condemnation of Molinos and Madame Guyon that he wrote the *Maxims of the Saints* in defence of the doctrine of Pure Love and of the mystical union. To him self-love was the root of all evil, and only those who became strangers to the Self, the I, could become the Friends of God and enter into intimacy with Him. His enemies secured his condemnation, but they could

[1] *The Spiritual Guide* (ed. 1688), p. 179.

not quench his faith, and it was in his disgrace that
Fénelon wrote his *Spiritual Letters*, by which the
spirit of French mysticism was perpetuated and bore
fruit in the lives of other mystics of other lands than
France.

All the Christian mystics whom we have considered
so far belonged to the Catholic Church, which has
at most times provided a favourable atmosphere for
the growth of the highest type of Mysticism, but
Protestantism has also produced its mystics. One
of the earliest and most extraordinary of these was
Jacob Boehme (1575-1624), a poor shoemaker who
lived at Gorlitz, on the border between Saxony and
Silesia. From his childhood he was interested in
religious matters and read deeply of mystical literature.
Then one day the mystic vision was given to him,
of which he writes : " I saw and knew the Being of all
Beings, the Byss and the Abyss—the Descent and
Origin of the World and of all creatures through the
Divine Wisdom." It was not only to vision, but
to gnosis that he attained : " In this Light my spirit
suddenly saw through all, and in and by all the
creatures ; it knew God—Who He is and what His
Will is ; and suddenly in that Light my will was set
on by a mighty impulse to describe the Being of God."
He believed that not only had he beheld God, but in
that moment of vision had been given him also
complete knowledge of the Universe, and this he set
forth in his writings.

This visible, temporal, phenomenal universe is
derived from an invisible, eternal, real universe.
This ultimate Reality differentiates within into the
Divine Persons, and outwardly into the visible and
invisible worlds. In this manifestation the Divine

Unity displays two principles, Light and Darkness, Wrath and Love, Good and Evil, the principle of Light and Love and Goodness in God being perfectly revealed once for all in the Incarnation. The soul has an innate, divine capacity of response to this Light and Love, and to be " saved " is to be united with the Divine life and to die to the isolated self. Says Boehme : " His life has been brought into mine, so that I am atoned with Him in His Love." The way to this union was by self-annihilation. " If thou dost surrender thyself wholly, then thou art dead to thy own will, and Love will be the Life of thy nature. When thou art wholly gone forth from the creature and become nothing to all that is native and creature, then thou art in that Eternal One which is God Himself." [1]

Boehme's books were widely read, and it was plain that his message met a felt need. His aim was a revitalising of the Lutheran Church, the teaching of a philosophy which should point to a deeper, truer doctrine of God and His relation to man than was supplied by the current orthodoxy. He also was among the creative mystics, and we shall find that his influence was largely responsible for the development of Mysticism which took place during the seventeenth and eighteenth centuries in England.

One of the greatest of these English mystics was George Fox (1624–1691), whose influence was perhaps more far-reaching than that of any other mystical thinker in England, as far as succeeding generations were concerned, and there is no doubt that he was affected by Boehme's writings. He found himself alienated, at an early age, from the Church and its

[1] *The Supersensual Life,* pp. 27 ff.

ministers, and came to the conclusion that man could be saved, not by external means of help, but only by the " inner Light " which was to be found within him.  Every soul has this " Light " or " Seed " of God within it, and by obedience and surrender on the part of the soul this Light may be enabled to increase, and the soul may overcome its natural tendencies to sin and become the spiritual instrument of the living God.  " As people come into subjection to the Spirit of God," he says in his *Journal*, " they may come to know the hidden unity in the Eternal Being."

He himself had known the mystic experience which gave him certitude, and of it he writes : " Now was I come up in spirit, through the flaming sword, into the paradise of God.  All things were new—I knew nothing but pureness and innocency and righteousness, being renewed up into the image of God.  Great things did the Lord lead me into, and wonderful depths were opened unto me, beyond what can by words be declared." [1]  Fox now gave himself up to the task of preaching his message of a new practice of the Presence of God, and a new spiritualised Church.  He formed groups called at first " Children of the Light," who became the Society of Friends. These modern mystics hold that the preparation for the mystic union must be first self-surrender in the spirit of love, and then the inward hush, a waiting in silent expectancy for the voice of the Holy Spirit revealing God to the soul.

William Law (1686–1761) was a somewhat different type of mystic from Fox, though equally influenced by Boehme.  He was at first inclined to emphasise

[1] i. 95.

the ideal of mediæval mysticism, in regard to self-denial and negation, but later he asserted a more positive doctrine based on the direct inward relation of the soul with the invisible universe, and a sense of the community of all living things, as all being subject to the same law of perfect love. The only salvation is the Life of God in the soul, and there can be no true religion except in and by the Spirit of Love, which is God Himself living and working within the soul. But the soul must be made fit for the indwelling of God, by purification, by renunciation of all self-will and desire, having and being nothing except as God chooses for it. " The greatest humility, the most absolute resignation of our whole selves to God, is our greatest and highest fitness to receive our greatest and highest purification from God." He has no doubt of the possibility of union in this life for those who are prepared to pay the price ; indeed, this unitive life he feels to be a necessity for those who seek to do God's will on earth ; the indwelling, the union, the working of the Deity within the life of the creature is as necessary for a good life as respiration is for animal life. By this union the creature will be transformed into the likeness of the Creator. " The Word of God is the hidden treasure of every human soul, immured under flesh and blood, till as a day-star it arises in our hearts and changes the son of an earthly Adam into a son of God."

It was by his books, and chiefly by *The Spirit of Love* and *The Spirit of Prayer*, that Law influenced those who came after him, including the Evangelical leaders.

The Mysticism of the seventeenth century in England had its effect upon the poetry of the period, and John

Donne, George Herbert, Crashaw, Traherne and
Henry Vaughan all shew the mystical tendency in
their poetry. Traherne writes in the true spirit of
the mystic in his poem on *The Vision* :

> " From one, to one, in one to see all things,
>     To see the King of kings,
> But once in two ; to see His endless treasures
>     Made all mine own, myself the end
> Of all his labours ! 'Tis the life of pleasures !
>     To see myself His friend !
> Who all things finds conjoined in Him alone,
>     Sees and enjoys the Holy One."

But greater than these were the poet-mystics of
the eighteenth and nineteenth centuries, the first of
whom was William Blake (1757–1827), the mystic
who sought to convey his teaching not only in words
but in form and colour. His greatest mystical poem
is " Jerusalem," in which he writes of self-annihilation,
of the death which leads to Resurrection and to life
in Unity, when all who shall return unto God shall
awake in His Bosom to the Life of Immortality,
poured out to them from the Wine-Press of Love.

Wordsworth (1770–1850) is a nature-mystic, who
in his contemplation of the creatures felt his oneness
with their Creator, and whose poetry is full of the
mystic sense of the Presence of God. In his *Prelude*
he writes of it thus :

>                         " With bliss ineffable,
> I felt the sentiment of Being spread
> O'er all that moves and all that seemeth still,
> O'er all that, lost beyond the reach of thought
> And human knowledge, to the human eye
> Invisible, yet liveth to the heart."

Robert Browning (1812–1889) was also a mystic, believing in a perfect spiritual world, towards which we look, and in a universe ruled by Love, the essence of which is self-sacrifice. In *Pauline* he describes the quest of the human soul :

> " What is it that I hunger for but God ?
> My God, my God ! let me for once look on Thee
> As though nought else existed : we alone.
> And as creation crumbles, my soul's spark
> Expands till I can say, Even from myself
> I need Thee, and I feel Thee and I love Thee."

God, to him, dwells within the soul, as He dwells in all existence, and the mystic gnosis, which shall lead to union with Him—

> " Rather consists in opening out a way
> Whence the imprisoned Splendour may escape
> Than in effecting entry for a light
> Supposed to be without." [1]

When the soul, in perfect love, gives itself wholly to the power of God within it, then shall God " embrace " it in the joy of lover and Love united not to part again.

[1] *Paracelsus.*

# EPILOGUE

THE mystics have given us their witness to the truth of the faith they hold ; philosophers have set their seal to it, the Fathers of the Church have affirmed their belief in it ; the seekers of the Orient have proclaimed in glowing terms their mystic creed ; those devoted to the Religious life have found in Mysticism that which brings vital force to dogmatic theology ; those who have lived in seclusion, together with those who have shared in all the activities of the busy world, men and women, saints and seers, poets and craftsmen, all alike have declared unfalteringly that the soul, already in this life, can and does enter consciously into immediate relationship with God. Have they justified their claim ?

Have they not rather justified it beyond all denial ? Their testimony bears on the face of it the evidence of being founded on experience ; they speak not by hearsay, but of that which they have seen and known for themselves. These mystics are no mere visionaries, unreliable witnesses, but men and women of strong character, possessed of sound judgment, and for the most part of practical good sense. They were known far and wide for the sanctity of their lives, the saintliness of their characters. Often they were profound thinkers, the intellectual leaders of their fellows, and withal men and women of action, with great gifts for leadership and administration, who have made their mark in the history of religion and oftentimes in the history of the world. Their inward vision did not make them less capable of serving their fellow-men, rather it inspired them to a fuller and richer life for others in the world. Their mysticism was a death opening up the gates of life, it was creative in the fullest sense of the word ; they were not content to abide alone, but in dying unto themselves they brought forth much fruit.

If we cannot follow them in the experience to which their mysticism led them, and cannot fully understand what they seek to tell us, we must remember that these inner experiences, these visions of Divine truth, are of their very nature indescribable and in-communicable. If but few can share in that mystic experience, it is perhaps because few are prepared to pay the price which the mystics have paid and to follow in their steps along the Mystic Way, for they have told us plainly that the Way is long and hard, and those who would attain must be ready to die completely to Self in order to live unto God. Yet we may learn from them and gain something for ourselves from their revelations, for our own guidance and encouragement, if we should seek to share, in however small a measure, in that which they enjoyed in its fullness ; they have at any rate shewn us the way, and whither it leads for those who will tread it unfalteringly till the end is achieved.

Are the mystics right, then ? I think we can but answer Yes, if Mysticism means the transcending of the temporal and the material for the sake of communion, even of union, with the Abiding and the Real ; if it means dying to the old life of the natural man, with all its limitations and desires, in order to attain to the freedom of a new supernatural Life which is everlasting ; if, in short, it means a real experience, here and now, of what we call Eternity.

# BIBLIOGRAPHY

Abelson, J., *Jewish Mysticism*.  London, 1913.

Augustine, St., Confessions of.  London, 1886.

Barnett, L. W., *Mahābhārata (Bhagavad-Gītā)*.  London, 1920.

Bernard, St., *The Love of God* (tr. M. C. and C. Patmore).  London, 1884.

Browne, E. G., " *Sūfism* " in *Religious Systems of the World*.  London, 1876.

Butler, C., *Western Mysticism*.  London, 1922.

*Cloud of Unknowing, The*, ed. E. Underhill.  London, 1912.

Conybeare, F. C., *Philo about the Contemplative Life*.  Oxford, 1895.

Davids, Mrs. R., *Buddhism*.  London, 1914.

Douglas, R. K., *Confucianism and Taoism*.  London, 1889.

*Francis, St., Little Flowers of* (tr. T. W. Arnold).  London, 1908.

Gardner, E., *St. Catherine of Siena*.  London, 1907.

—— *The Cell of Self-Knowledge*.  London, 1907.

Giles, L., *The Sayings of Lao-tzŭ*.  London, 1913.

Graham, J. C., *St. Teresa, her Life and Times*.  London, 1907.

Hilton, Walter, *The Scale of Perfection*, ed. E. Underhill.  London, 1923.

Hügel, F. von, *The Mystical Element of Religion*.  London, 1923.

—— *Eternal Life*.  London, 1912.

Inge, W. R., *Christian Mysticism*.  London, 1899.

—— *Light, Life and Love*.  London, 1919.

John of the Cross, St., *The Flame of Living Love* (tr. D. Lewis).  1912.

—— *The Dark Night of the Soul* (tr. D. Lewis).  1916.

Jones, R., *Studies in Mystical Religion*.  London, 1909.

Josephus, F., *Works* (tr. W. Whiston).  London, 1811.

Julian of Norwich, *Revelations of Divine Love*, ed. G. Warrack.  London, 1901.

Kennedy, H. A. A., *St. Paul and the Mystery Religions*. London, 1913.

Neander, A., *Church History* (tr. J. Torrey). Edinburgh, 1851.

Nicholson, R. A., *The Mystics of Islām*. London, 1914.

Petrie, W. M. Flinders, *Egypt and Israel*. London, 1913.

Pfleiderer, O., *Primitive Christianity* (tr. W. Montgomery). London, 1910.

Plato, *The Dialogues* (tr. Jowett). Oxford, 1892.

—— *The Republic* (tr. Jowett). Oxford, 1888.

Plotinus, *The Enneads*, 5 Vols. (tr. S. Mackenna). London, 1917.

Rolle, R., *The Fire of Love and the Mending of Life*, ed. F. Comper. London, 1914.

Ruysbroeck, John of, *The Adornment of the Spiritual Marriage*, *The Book of Truth*, and *Book of the Sparkling Stone* (tr. P. Wynschenk Dom). London, 1916.

*Sepher ha-Zohar* (tr. J. de Pauly). Paris, 1906.

Sharpe, A. B., *Mysticism, its true Nature and Value*. London, 1910.

Smith, M., *Rābi'a the Mystic and her Fellow-Saints in Islām*. Cambridge, 1928.

*Suso, Life of* (tr. T. F. Knox). London, 1913.

Tauler, J., *Twenty-five Sermons* (tr. S. Winkworth). London, 1906.

*Theologia Germanica* (tr. S. Winkworth). London, 1907.

Underhill, E., *Mysticism*. London, 1912.

—— *Mystics of the Church*. London, 1925.

# INDEX